Fabrics
For
Historic
Buildings

Jane C. Nylander

The Preservation Press

National Trust
for Historic Preservation

Author Jane C. Nylander is Curator of Textiles and Ceramics at Old Sturbridge Village, Mass.

The National Trust for Historic Preservation, chartered by Congress in 1949, is the only private, nonprofit organization with the responsibility to encourage public participation in the preservation of sites, buildings and objects significant in American history and culture. Support is provided by membership dues, endowment funds and contributions and by matching grants from federal agencies, including the U.S. Department of the Interior, National Park Service, under provisions of the National Historic Preservation Act of 1966.

THE PRESERVATION PRESS 1977
National Trust for Historic Preservation
740-748 Jackson Place, N.W.
Washington, D.C.   20006

Cover: Bruton Resist, an F. Schumacher & Co. Colonial Williamsburg Reproduction of an 18th-century document. Document color approximated. See page 25 and figure 15.

Contents

Fabrics for Historic Buildings   5
Why Use Reproductions?   6
Documentary Research Prior to Fabric Selection   6
Selecting Reproduction Fabrics   8
Custom Reproduction Work   9
Construction and Installation of Fabric Furnishings   10

CATALOGUE   12

Documentary Reproduction Fabrics
The Eighteenth Century   13
 Reproductions of 18th-Century Fabrics:
 Wools   14
 Checks and Stripes   16
 Prints   17
 Woven Silk Designs   26
1790-1815: Changing Taste and Technology   32
 Reproductions of 1790-1815 Fabrics:
 Prints   33
 Woven Designs   39
1815-1840: Technological Changes and Complex Designs   40
 Reproductions of 1815-40 Fabrics:
 Prints   41
 Woven Designs   42
1840-1870: Popularity in Fabric Furnishings   44
 Reproductions of 1840-70 Fabrics:
 Prints   44
 Woven Designs   45
 Embroideries   48
1870-1900: Complexity and Variety   49
 Reproductions of 1870-1900 Fabrics   49

Nondocumentary and Plain Woven Fabrics   53

Manufacturers   57

Glossary   59

Selected Bibliography   63

1. Bed hangings of <u>Peel Document</u>, reproduction fabric by Waverly, in the Salem Towne House at Old Sturbridge Village, Mass. The design of the early 19th-century hangings is taken from an original set with 41 separate pieces that is in the Essex Institute, Salem, Mass. Also see figure 26 and page 37. (Old Sturbridge Village Photo, Donald F. Eaton)

Fabrics for Historic Buildings

Furnishing fabrics--curtains, upholstery, bed hangings--are a fundamental part of the restoration or period interpretation of a historic building. Because textiles are more perishable and more frequently updated than building materials, modern reproductions are often the most authentic fabrics available. This book is written to aid persons with limited fabric experience in the selection and ordering of reproduction fabrics and other fabrics suitable for furnishing historic properties. It addresses basic historical, curatorial and practical considerations, but it is not intended to substitute for careful study of period documents, of well-researched secondary sources and of reproduction fabrics themselves.

The catalogue section of the book lists reproductions of fabrics used in the United States between the 18th century and 1900. It is organized by period and to some extent by type. Brief discussions of fabric furnishings that character-ized each period are provided as a general guide to the evolution of fabric design and use. These discussions should be supplemented by appropriate sources listed in the bibliography (p. 63). The glossary (p. 59) is likewise included as a general aid that should be expanded in the context of a particular period by additional reading.

The substance of the catalogue section is the specific information it provides for selecting and ordering commercial reproduction fabrics. The information is current as of January 1, 1977. Most of the details were provided by the manu-facturers listed on page 57, companies highly regarded for the quality of their products. Because fabric companies change their offerings as often as once a year, retaining successful patterns and discontinuing those that do not sell well or that present production difficulties, the reader should keep in mind that some fabrics listed in this book may be discontinued and that new patterns will be added. It is important to note that manufacturers often keep the print-ing screens and weaving patterns when styles are discontinued, and in such cases it may be possible to obtain the fabric by special order.

The catalogue sections are an index to the current availability of reproduction fabrics and do not represent a typical sampling of the fabrics used in the United States at any period in history. Many of the reproduction fabrics ori-ginally were commissioned for specific restoration projects, and they reflect specific interests. Designs and materials suitable for sophisticated structures of the 18th and early 19th centuries predominate over reproductions appropriate for more modest settings and for later periods. For example, the most common 18th-century fabric for bed and window hangings and upholstery was wool. The texture and finish of woolen cloth has changed so drastically in the last 200 years that most modern wools are unsuitable for use in a period context unless made specifically as period reproductions, and there are few of these. In con-trast, many French, English, Italian and Indian designs in silks or cotton prints have been reproduced faithfully and are offered in tempting variety.

Why Use Reproductions?

Should one be concerned with fabric reproductions if there is original fabric available? Period designs usually call for so much yardage that the use of antique textiles would be impossible. In cases when such use would be possible, such as when original curtains or ample original yardage have survived, preservation of the original materials should be the primary goal. In most cases these original fabrics have survived only because they have been carefully protected from light, dirt and insect attack; sudden exposure can only hasten their destruction. There are virtually no circumstances that justify the damage caused to original textiles by exposure to light and dust for long periods of time.

Display of certain antique textile items, such as quilts or other bed coverings, may be acceptable on a short-term basis, provided there is some control of light in the room. If original objects cannot be rotated regularly, a reproduction should be substituted for everyday display. In no case should original objects be left out for long periods of time.

The practice of cutting up original bed curtains, bedspreads, quilts, coverlets and other artifacts for curtains or upholstery also should be avoided totally. Such uses are historically inaccurate as well as destructive. Even cutting up old linen sheets for use as curtains or the base of embroideries is unacceptable. It is also impractical: The weakened fibers will not long survive and the new work will be lost.

The use of reproduction fabrics, therefore, allows the preservation of original documents while recreating authentic period effects. An additional benefit of using reproductions is that the fabrics can be cleaned by modern commercial methods and can be replaced when necessary to maintain the freshness of colors and appearance.

A documentary reproduction fabric is a modern textile that copies as accurately as possible a historic original or document. In some cases fabrics that are not specifically termed documentary reproductions are also suitable for restoration work. Some mid or late 19th-century designs have never been discontinued. In addition, plain woven fabrics of pure fibers that have changed little over time are still available from a variety of commercial sources. Machine technology has, of course, sometimes produced alterations in width and texture, but by and large these are acceptable. The catalogue section of this book cites some specific examples and sources of nondocumentary fabrics for restoration work.

Documentary Research Prior to Fabric Selection

A common mistake in restoration work has been to neglect preliminary documentary research and instead arbitrarily to select a date for restoration (often the date of original construction of the building) and then look for beautiful designs and materials appropriate to the chosen period. Some of the interiors created by this procedure would probably astonish their original owners, who might never have dreamed of having silk draperies made from designs published in Paris the year they were married.

Few projects will have the documentary evidence and surviving material to assure accurate restoration to a single early date. The selection of a broad time frame, on the other hand, opens up a considerable range of choices. For example, in what style does one curtain an 18th-century house in which most of the furniture dates from the middle years of the 19th century and which has been continuously lived in by the same family to the early years of the 20th century? Or, what does one do with an otherwise Federal style interior if original curtains survive from the 1870s? What if the room function has changed? The choice of appropriate furnishings grows out of a comprehensive understanding of the property and its occupants, one that expands rather than limits the impression of the whole.

The first task in selecting fabrics for use in historic interiors is to establish clearly the purpose of the restoration and the extent and quality of existing documentation. The adequacy of documentary evidence may in fact determine whether the restoration is to emphasize an exact date or a broad time frame. If samples of original textile material (or written descriptions of colors and fabrics or early photographs or even drawings) have survived, then one should consider whether it is desirable to recreate a specific moment in the history of a particular room or building. If so, the search for commercially available reproductions that approximate the surviving documents can begin. It is also possible to consider ordering custom reproductions.

If, on the other hand, there is no evidence about the use of earlier furnishing textiles, what does one do? The first step is to undertake research in primary sources specifically related to the house and to similar houses in the same geographic area. These sources include inventories, diaries, letters, account books, photographs, paintings, newspapers, design books, advice books and magazines. It is important to know as much as possible about the interior involved before any decisions are made. Some questions to ask are: How old is the building? Who built it? What purpose did it serve? How was each room used? If it is a house, how many people lived there? How old were they? When were they married? How many children did they have? How long did their descendants live there? Was this their first house? When was it remodeled and why? At what economic level within the community were the owners? Did they purchase things locally? If not, did they order things from a commercial supplier or did they travel themselves? If so, where did they go? What might they have seen? In other words, what sources of fabric and design were available to the owners within their known geographic and economic limitations? The answers to such questions will guide the researcher in gathering information and making decisions.

With the intent of the restoration determined and the historical research carefully done, decisions can then be made about the period to be represented. Since the furnishing fabrics will be a major factor in recreating a period effect, the importance of selecting the fabrics and using them in proper context cannot be overemphasized. If possible, it is desirable to study original textiles from the selected period before choosing a reproduction fabric. Becoming familiar with the appearance of original textiles also gives one a better basis for judging the accuracy of reproduction work. Many major art museums and historical societies maintain textile study collections that can be viewed by appointment. A good source for locating collections in a particular geographic area or with a given specialty is Cecil Lubell's Textile Collections of the World: United States and Canada.

If it is not possible to examine original textiles firsthand, one should at least study details of design and printing illustrated in published sources. Probably the most helpful books are Florence Montgomery's Printed Textiles, the Victoria and Albert Museum's English Printed Textiles: Large Picture Book No. 13 and Clouzot and Morris, Printed and Painted Fabrics. It is also possible to order detailed photographs of original fabrics from textile study collections. There is no substitute for seeing the original example, however, for details and texture cannot be conveyed accurately by photograph, and lens distortion may be misleading.

Selecting Reproduction Fabrics

The choice of a reproduction fabric should be guided by the results of historical research, but it should be understood that, no matter how expensive and how carefully supervised, fabric produced by modern methods will not exactly duplicate the original appearance of its historical counterpart and that exact duplication is not always the primary goal. In addition, each project will have specific economic and technical requirements that must be considered. Before attempting to choose among the fairly large selection of documentary reproduction fabrics currently on the market, it is crucial to define the variations from the original that are acceptable for the given project.

One might assume that the fiber must always be the same--that silk originals should be reproduced in silk, wool in wool, cotton in cotton. The possibility of using synthetic yarns, however, is likely to arise when the costs of silk or wool are considered and the durability of synthetics is compared to that of natural fibers. Victoria Damask by Brunschwig & Fils (p. 48) is a modern reproduction in rayon, cotton and wool that achieves substantially the texture of the original wool drapery fabric. Those responsible for a restoration will have to decide whether they can afford the most technically accurate reproduction possible or if a reasonably exact duplication of visual effect is what is sought.

In choosing a reproduction fabric, one should be aware of differences caused by the changing technology of textile production during the past 200 years. In no case can modern commercial spinning and weaving processes duplicate the appearance or texture of hand-production methods, nor can chemical dyes exactly duplicate the colors achieved by vegetable dyes. The silk-screen and steel-roller printing and the photoengraving methods that are often used for reproductions cannot exactly duplicate the visual effects of the original block or copperplate printing or of hand engraving. Some reproductions using these methods do remarkably well, but inevitably some detail is lost.

The standard loom sizes have also changed, so that modern warps are longer and widths are greater than those of earlier periods. In some cases the original designs can be printed double to fit the wider cloth, but more often they must be adjusted slightly in order to produce a unified design. Sometimes large copperplate designs cannot be reworked into modern widths; in those cases, the original design may be reproduced with large unprinted areas at the sides.

The texture of goods selected for printing or of yarns for woven designs is crucial to the success of a reproduction. One should be aware that the original document has probably lost body through wear and cleaning. On the other hand, if too coarse a texture is selected for printed designs, design detail will be lost. Slubs, or lumps on threads, which in the past were regarded as undesirable imperfections in spinning, should not be arbitrarily added to modern goods in an attempt to make them look old. Similarly, reproduction of faded color or of discoloration, known as aged grounds, does a disservice to a design that was originally printed on a white ground.

The use of undocumented colors is inappropriate in restoration work. In most commercial reproduction fabrics, the color of the original is reproduced and designated the document color, such as document blue or document red or documentary colorway. Some reproductions are available in nondocumentary colors as well, in which case the original color is often listed as number 1 in the catalogue code number series for that fabric. The Colonial Williamsburg line by F. Schumacher & Co. is an example of documentary reproductions that are also available in other colors not necessarily of the period. Sometimes the other colors available may have been possible historically, but in most cases the modern colors were unknown in the past and could not have been created with the dye technology then in use. An accurate restoration project must be designed within the framework of the contemporary technology, no matter how repetitious or strange it may seem.

It happens sometimes that an acceptable reproduction is entirely inappropriate for use as a furnishing fabric because the document would not have been used that way originally. For example, one of F. Schumacher & Co.'s Colonial Williamsburg reproductions, Country Linen, is based on an American 18th-century handwoven linen grain sack. In addition to the documentary natural fibers, it is available in several colors, described as "a modern fabric with traditional texture and quality." This is an attractive fabric for a variety of decorative effects, but grain sacks were probably never used for furnishing fabrics. Always establish that the reproduction fabric could have been used in the restoration context intended.

When writing to a manufacturer to request a catalogue, be sure to specify that it is for historic restoration purposes. Some manufacturers will provide samples for restoration projects on request, and samples are also sometimes available through local decorators. Before contacting a manufacturer, it is advisable to (1) assemble all data and photographs pertinent to the restoration, as well as any available original fabrics and (2) complete preliminary restoration plans, including specific requirements such as the period to be recreated, the full measurements of all surfaces to be covered, the projected use of the room and the projected work schedule. When ordering goods, be sure to request a current run cutting, which is a sample of the color currently available, in order to be assured that it is the same color as that of the sample originally approved. Check the cutting for the quality of printing also; worn-out screens produce heavy blots of color that are not desirable. When an order is received, examine the entire yardage for any flaws that would make it unacceptable.

Custom Reproduction Work

If one seeks the most exact possible reproduction of a specific prototype, it is usually necessary to enter into negotiations for the custom manufacture of a limited amount of yardage and the accompanying trimmings. (It is also possible, and somewhat less expensive, to obtain special color runs of currently available designs.) There is a frequent misunderstanding among historic house restoration committees with carefully cherished samples of original fabric that by offering a sample to a company for inclusion in its commercial line, the company will in turn provide the restoration with "all the fabric they need" and a handsome royalty. Occasionally it may indeed be possible to convince a manufacturer to include a special design as part of the regular commercial line, paying a royalty at stated intervals. In that case the costs are considerably less, but this rarely occurs. It is wiser to approach custom work with the clear-eyed expectation that it will be very expensive and that the company is really doing you a favor to work to your exacting specifications.

In order for custom work to be done, it is usually necessary for the client to bear the expenses of setting up the looms and of reproducing the original color and design as well as the expenses of materials and labor. Price may vary depending on the yardage required, small amounts of yardage being the most expensive. In most cases, a 50 percent deposit is required. Negotiation for custom reproduction work is inevitably a highly personal experience. Among the few companies that are willing to undertake custom work on a limited basis are Scalamandrè, Brunschwig & Fils, Clarence House and Old World Weavers. All are experienced in working with museums and can be commended for their cooperative attitude and excellent workmanship.

Signing a contract and paying a deposit are only the first steps in a long process. It can sometimes take 16 to 18 months for a company to finish a custom-woven product. It is wise to check on the work at every step of production, approving actual samples and color strikeoffs. Modern production methods and dyestuffs are not the same as those that produced the original, and it is not wise to assume that there will be a flawless result. The client has the right to insist on as perfect a reproduction of the original as possible, with full understanding and approval of any changes that are made by the company. There will often be delays in the expected delivery time. For these or other reasons, there may be increased charges, so it is wise to determine in advance if the price estimate represents a maximum charge or if allowance should be made for inflationary cost increases. Be sure to have firm price estimates in hand when seeking funds or to allot a percentage of the budget for possible cost overruns.

The manufacturer may recommend that a certain percentage of additional goods be ordered at the outset to compensate for possible flaws. No manufacturer will make adjustments for imperfections once goods have been cut, and it is imperative to examine the entire yardage when it is first received.

Construction and Installation of Fabric Furnishings

Once the reproduction fabrics have been chosen, a number of questions remain. In actually making up the goods, one must decide on the degree of accuracy to which the reproduction furnishing must adhere. If an original curtain or bedspread was handstitched, unlined and perhaps fastened with iron tacks, should the modern reproduction be machine sewn, lined and fastened with Velcro? In deciding, one should remember the original purpose of the restoration. If a decorative effect is the major goal, by all means choose the best modern construction and installation methods. The fabrics will last longer and be much easier to clean. If, on the other hand, the interpretation of a way of life at a given moment is the goal, the completed work should be as absolutely faithful to the original as possible. To achieve this, all stitching should be a close approximation of the size and type of hand or machine work done on original examples. Lining should be employed only if there is a prototype, and original hanging methods should be duplicated if at all possible. When such practical details are not available in published sources, one must seek them through careful study of existing documents and published designs and illustrations from the period.

2. Window hung with <u>Marlboro Cotton</u> by Brunschwig, c. 1805-07, in the Marlboro Room, Henry Francis du Pont Winterthur Museum, Winterthur, Del.

CATALOGUE

This catalogue of fabrics suitable for restoration work is divided into two parts. The first deals with documentary reproduction fabrics; it is arranged by historical period. The second part deals with nondocumentary and plain woven fabrics; it is arranged by type. Individual catalogue entries give the following information when available:

Manufacturer's catalogue name for fabric

Place, date and method of manufacture of the original

Citation for published photograph of document fabric (see bibliography for complete titles)

Fiber content of the reproduction fabric

Width of the fabric/Length of one complete pattern motif

Changes made in reproduction

Organization or museum for which the fabric was reproduced

Information about the document and location of document

Manufacturer's catalogue number for the fabric

Manufacturer's name for the document color (The word series following a catalogue number means that the fabric is available in more than one color and that the manufacturer has not specified the document color. Some of the colors available may not be of the period.)

The manufacturers' complete names and addresses are given on page 57.

Documentary Reproduction Fabrics

The Eighteenth Century

Imported fabrics seem to have been preferred for furnishing American buildings in the 18th century. English fabrics, protected by the high taxes that the mother country imposed on goods imported into the colonies from other countries, predominated.

The 18th century saw the beginnings of industrialization in textile manufacture in England. Throughout the period designs were hand-printed from woodblocks, but in the middle of the century the introduction of mechanical processes and engraved copper plates for printing on cotton or linen expanded production and made possible fine linear designs with much larger repeats that were especially well adapted for furnishing use. The colors were primarily deep indigo blues and the rich purples, reds and sepias that are derived from madder. Typical English designs included large-scale flowers and birds, chinoiseries, pastoral landscapes and special commemorative designs.

By the late 1770s copperplate printing began to be developed in France, especially by C. P. Oberkampf at Jouy. His work reached such a level of quality that the term toiles de Jouy, meaning cottons printed at Jouy, has become almost a generic term for copperplate printed textiles. After the American Revolution these French designs were imported to the United States and used as furnishing fabrics.

In addition to improvements and mechanization in spinning, weaving and printing, the late 18th century saw the beginning of experimentation with dye technology. In some cases, additional colors were "penciled" or added with woodblocks to the monochromatic copperplate designs. It was not until 1814, however, that a good green could be printed in one step. Before that time blue and yellow were overprinted to make green, and if the print was out of register, blue and yellow showed at the edges of all green areas. Frequently, the yellow dyes were not as fast as the blue; consequently many surviving floral printed textiles now appear to have blue stems and leaves. In most cases these were originally green, but because of the fugitive nature of the yellow they now appear blue. Reproductions of such fabrics should duplicate the original green.

Documentary evidence makes it clear that few houses were embellished with elaborate window hangings in the colonial period. For those who could afford domestic luxury, the most lavish use of fabrics was in the covering and hanging of the best bed. In many estate inventories, the value of beds with hangings far exceeds that of any other piece of furniture in the entire house. Bed hangings of green harrateen or cheyney were common, with crimson or scarlet the second most popular color. (See Abbott Lowell Cummings, Bed Hangings, p. 14.) If there were any window hangings at all, they would have been hung in the parlor chamber, the room over the parlor where the best bed was located. Usually the fabric and color of the curtains matched that of the bed hangings. Any upholstered furniture or window-seat cushions in the room were usually covered in the same material or in leather of the same color. Slipcovers or cases of printed or checked cotton or linen were frequently used to protect the upholstery. If a family had curtains in more than one room, the second set would be in the parlor. Occasionally there were window hangings also in a family sitting room and in one or two secondary bedchambers.

Those responsible for recreating colonial interiors have available a tempting and at the same time a misleading choice of fabrics. There are many excellent reproductions of 18th-century silks, linens and printed cottons, but limited evidence to support their use in American buildings. Wool, by far the most commonly used material, is scarcely represented among modern reproduction fabrics. Where restoration research indicates the use of domestic wool or linen fabric that would have been handwoven, it is fairly easy to have hand-woven reproductions made. See Constance Dann Gallagher, Linen Heirlooms; also, for natural dyes of the period, Rita Adrosko, Natural Dyes and Home Dyeing.

REPRODUCTIONS OF 18th-CENTURY FABRICS

WOOLS

BRUNSCHWIG & FILS, INC.

Moreen Wool Texture. 18th or 19th century. 100% wool. 48" wide (no centerfold). Available plain or embossed. Reproduced for the Metropolitan Museum of Art, New York City, and the Museum of Early Southern Decorative Arts, Winston-Salem, N.C. No. 38693.01 (document gold). No. 38696.01 (document coral). Fig. 3

Verplanck Damask. English or Flemish, probably late 18th century. 100% wool. 52" wide (2 panels of 20"), 57 1/2" repeat. Reproduced for the Metropolitan Museum of Art, New York City; used in the museum's Verplanck Room. Special order only. Fig. 4

SCALAMANDRÈ SILKS, INC.

Baize Cloth. English, 18th or early 19th century. 100% wool. 50" wide. Document at Independence National

Historical Park, Philadelphia. No. 99243 (green)

Embossed Moreen. French, 18th century. 25% linen, 50% wool, 17% cotton, 8% silk. 51" wide. Available either plain or with moiré design. No. 1945 (old red)

F. SCHUMACHER & CO.

Arnold Brocade. French, 18th century. 50% wool, 50% cotton. 54" wide, 7 3/4" repeat. Reproduced for the Preservation Society of Newport County, Newport, R.I. Document a silk damask in the Schumacher Collection. No. 20652 (red and gold)

F. SCHUMACHER & CO. Colonial Williamsburg Reproductions

Peyton Randolph Wool Damask. English, late 18th century. 100% wool. 52" wide, 23" repeat. Document at Colonial Williamsburg, Williamsburg, Va. No. 32910 series

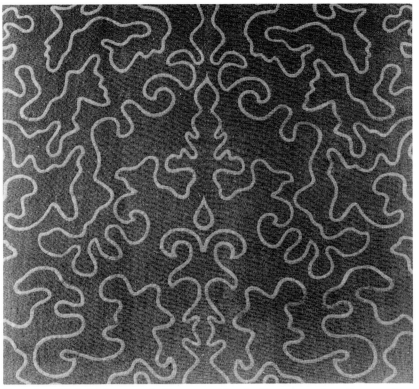

3. <u>Vermicelli Embossed Moreen Wool Texture</u> by Brunschwig,
    18th or early 19th century; photograph deliberately
    exaggerates the contrast of the embossed pattern

4. Chair upholstered in <u>Verplanck Damask</u> by
    Brunschwig, probably late 18th century, in
    the Verplanck Room, Metropolitan Museum of
    Art, New York City

Williamsburg Wool Satin. 100% wool. 52" wide. Document at Colonial Williamsburg. No. 82690 series

CHECKS AND STRIPES

F. SCHUMACHER & CO. Colonial Williamsburg Reproductions

Richmond Stripe. Late 18th century, woven. 72% mercerized cotton, 28% silk. 54" wide, 2" repeat. No. 20970 (document red)

Shir O Shakhar. 18th century, broad striped seersucker. 100% cotton. 54" wide, no repeat. No. 81570 series

Williamsburg Lateral Stripe. American, 18th century. 73% wool, 27% cotton. 54" wide, 3 3/4" repeat.

Document a tabby weave blanket. No. 81674 (blue, white and black)

Williamsburg Liner Stripe. English, c. 1750, block print. In Montgomery, Printed Textiles, figs. 2, 428 (top). 100% cotton. 50" wide. Originally fabrics such as this were cut into strips and used for border tapes, especially on bed quilts and curtains. Document owned by the New York Historical Society, New York City. No. 63113 (document red). Fig. 5

Wythe House Stripe. Late 18th century. 100% cotton. 50" wide, no repeat. No. 111342 (document two tone red)

Also see the reproduction checks on page 53

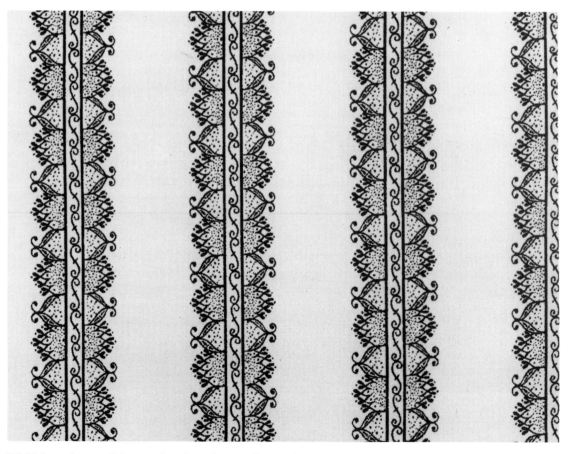

5. Williamsburg Liner Stripe by Schumacher, c. 1750

PRINTS

BRUNSCHWIG & FILS, INC.

Ballon de Gonesse. French (Jouy), 1784-85. In Clouzot, pl. XIV. 100% cotton. 39" wide, 38 1/2" repeat. Document at the Cooper-Hewitt Museum, New York City. No. 37251.01 (red)

Baroda. French, mid-18th century, multicolored arborescent block print. 48% cotton, 52% linen. 48" wide, 37" repeat. Document privately owned. No. 170320.00 (red, green, mauve on white ground)

Bird and Thistle (Walnut Room). English, c. 1790, copperplate print. In Montgomery, Printed Textiles, fig. 247. 100% cotton. 54" wide, 31 1/2" repeat. Document in the Henry Francis du Pont Winterthur Museum, Winterthur, Del. No. 65751.01 (red). Fig. 6

Bromelia Resist. English, c. 1765, resist-dyed cotton quilt with printed borders. In Montgomery, Printed Textiles, fig. 192. 100% cotton. 44" wide plus 2 1/2" border on each side, 29" repeat. Quilt top and border reproduced. Document in the Henry Francis du Pont Winterthur Museum, Winterthur, Del. No. 76862.04 (indigo). Fig. 7

Canton Resist. English or American, mid-18th century, resist print. 100% cotton. 54" wide, 28 1/2" repeat. Document in the Textile Study Room, Metropolitan Museum of Art, New York City. No. 73052.04 (indigo)

Chinoiserie Tree. English, c. 1750-70, block print. 100% linen. 54" wide, 65" repeat. Reproduced for the Henry Francis du Pont Winterthur Museum, Winterthur, Del. No. 72371.01 (crimson)

Climbing Roses. French (Orange), 1766. In Clouzot, pl. XL.

100% cotton. 54" wide, 21 1/4" repeat. Document in the Textile Study Room, Metropolitan Museum of Art, New York City. No. 76305.04 (white on pink)

Colbert. French (probably Nantes), mid-18th century, block print. 45% cotton, 55% linen. 48" wide, 11 1/2" repeat. Document in the Brunschwig Collection. No. 73570.04 (claret)

Deborah Logan. Indian, mid to late 18th century, block print. 100% cotton. 48" wide, 10 1/4" repeat. Document a quilt found at Stenton, Philadelphia. No. 73422.04 (indigo on off-white)

Duras Painted Taffetas. Chinese Export, probably 18th century. 100% silk. 48" wide, 25 1/2" repeat. Document in the Textile Study Room, Metropolitan Museum of Art, New York City. No. 39130.00 (multicolor on cream)

Georgian Serpentines. English, c. 1750, block printed and painted. 100% cotton. 48" wide, 22 3/4" repeat. Reproduced for the Textile Study Room, Metropolitan Museum of Art, New York City. Document window hangings used in the American Wing of the museum. No. 70750.04 (red and blue)

Grand Genois Panneau. Indian, mid-18th century, printed and painted palampore for the European market. 100% cotton. 63" wide, 91" repeat (cut by the panel). Document privately owned. No. 173490.00 (multicolor on white)

Hampton Resist. English, c. 1740-80, resist print. 56% cotton, 44% linen. 46" wide plus one 2" border on one side, 32 1/2" repeat. Reproduced for the Henry Francis du Pont Winterthur Museum, Winterthur, Del. No. 77312.04 (blue)

Homage d'Amérique Toile. French (Jouy), c. 1786, copperplate print showing France congratulating America on her

6. <u>Bird and Thistle</u> (Walnut Room) by Brunschwig, c. 1790

7. <u>Bromelia Resist</u> by Brunschwig, c. 1765

independence, designed by Jean Baptiste Huet. In Clouzot, pl. XXV. 100% cotton. 39" wide, 37 3/4" repeat. Document in the Brunschwig Collection. No. 37421.01 (red on white). Fig. 8

Kandahar Print, Kandahar Border. French, mid-18th century, madder and indigo block print. 100% cotton. Print 31" wide, 54 3/4" repeat; border 15 1/2" wide, 31 1/2" repeat. Document owned by manufacturer at Oberkampf, Alsace, France. No. 172300.00 (print, multicolor on cream), 172310.00 (border, multicolor on cream)

La Pagode Toile. French (Jouy or Nantes), c. 1786, copperplate print. In Clouzot, pl. LXII. 100% cotton. 39" wide, 37 3/4" repeat. Document at the Cooper-Hewitt Museum, New York City. No. 35082.01 (blue). Fig. 9

La Valette. Indian, early 18th century, printed and painted cotton for the European market. 100% cotton. 40" wide, 13 1/2" repeat. Hand blocked. Document privately owned. No. 172750.00 (multicolor on cream)

La Vallière. French, mid-18th century, resist dyed. 55% cotton, 45% linen. 39" wide, 25" repeat. Document in the Victoria and Albert Museum, London. No. 37412.01 (indigo on white)

L'Eventail. French (Jouy), c. 1785, block print. 100% cotton. 50" wide, 5" repeat. Document privately owned. No. 173224.00 (green)

Mirande. French, c. 1785-90, block print. 100% cotton. 48" wide, 16" repeat. Document privately owned. No. 37510.01 (cream ground)

Nepal. Indian, late 18th century, madder and indigo painted cotton.

100% cotton. 55" wide, 19 1/4" repeat. Document privately owned. No. 173661.00 (red and blue on cream). Fig. 10

Peony Tree. English, c. 1780, block print. In Montgomery, Printed Textiles, fig. 81. 100% cotton. 54" wide, 36" repeat. Reproduced for the Henry Francis du Pont Winterthur Museum, Winterthur, Del. No. 73231.04 (madder and indigo)

Philadelphia Stripe. American (Philadelphia), 1775 or 1776, block print by Walters and Bedwell, the earliest identified signed product of an American textile printer. 100% linen. 50" wide including 2" overmatch, 9 1/4" repeat. Reproduced for the Henry Francis du Pont Winterthur Museum, Wintherthur, Del. Document at the museum. No. 73818.04 (brown and rose). Fig. 11

Poligny Toile. French (Jouy), c. 1780, copperplate print. 100% cotton. 35" wide, 35" repeat. Document in the Brunschwig Collection. No. 67242.01 (blue)

Powhatan Toile. French, c. 1785, block print. 100% cotton. 52" wide, 15" repeat. Reproduced for the Valentine Museum, Richmond, Va. Document in the Brunschwig Collection. No. 77661.04 (red and green)

Prancing Deer. English, c. 1750-80, resist print. 56% cotton, 44% linen. 46" wide plus one 2" border on one side, 32 1/2" repeat. Reproduced for the Henry Francis du Pont Winterthur Museum, Winterthur, Del. Document a coverlet in the Winterthur Museum. No. 77312.04 (blue)

Sikar. Indian, mid-18th century, hand painted. 100% cotton. 50" wide, 20" repeat. Document privately owned. No. 172910.00 (multicolor on cream)

Srinagar. Indian, mid-18th century, hand painted. 100% cotton. 31" wide,

8. Homage d'Amérique Toile by Brunschwig, c. 1786

9. La Pagode Toile by Brunschwig, c. 1786

10. <u>Nepal</u> by Brunschwig, late 18th century

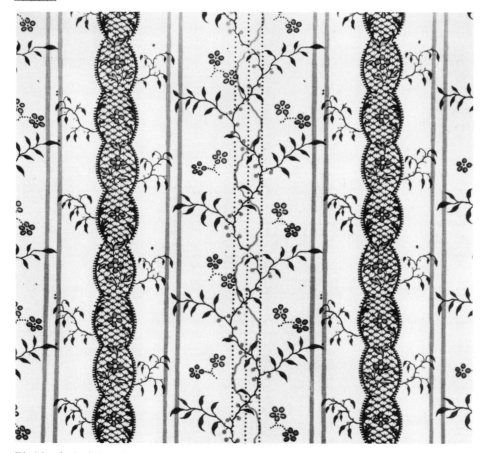

11. <u>Philadelphia Stripe</u> by Brunschwig, 1775 or 1776

12. <u>Resist Print</u> by Scalamandrè, c. 1776 (James Vincent)

13. <u>China Blue</u> by Greeff, c. 1750 (Richard Dillon, Jr.)

27 1/2" repeat. Document privately owned. No. 172700.00 (multicolor on cream)

Toile D'Inde. Indian, mid-18th century, block print probably for the English market. 100% cotton. 48" wide, 18 3/4" repeat. Reproduced for the Museum of Early Southern Decorative Arts, Winston-Salem, N.C. No. 75400.04 (red and green)

Toile Dupleix. Indian, late 18th century, madder and indigo block print probably for the European market. 100% cotton. 51" wide, 46" repeat. Document in the Victoria and Albert Museum, London. No. 173640.00 (multicolor on white)

Villandry. French (Jouy), c. 1785, block print. 100% cotton. 48" wide, 6" repeat. Document in the Brunschwig Collection. No. 72151.04 (red)

Villefranche. French, c. 1785, resist dyed. 45% cotton, 55% linen. 48" wide, 26 1/2" repeat. Document in the Brunschwig Collection. No. 75301.04 (red)

GREEFF FABRICS, INC.

China Blue. English, c. 1750, block print. 100% cotton. 56" wide, 32 1/2" repeat. Document a bedspread and bed hangings in the Essex Institute, Salem, Mass. No. 58842 (blue on natural). Fig. 13

SCALAMANDRÈ SILKS, INC.

Flower Basket. English, c. 1770-80, resist print. In Montgomery, Printed Textiles, fig. 189. 100% linen. 50" wide, 17 1/2" repeat. Adaptation from a document in the textile collection at the Metropolitan Museum of Art, New York City. No. 6412-2 (blue on ecru)

French Resist. French, mid-18th century, resist print. 44% linen, 56% cotton. 48" wide, 22" repeat. Screen-printed adaptation from a document in the textile collection at the Metropolitan Museum of Art, New York City. No. 6410-1 (indigo on natural)

Italian Countryside. French (Jouy), c. 1775-90, copperplate print from design by Jean Baptiste Huet. 100% cotton. 50" wide, 35 3/4" repeat. Document in the Scalamandrè Collection. No. 6411-1 (blue on white)

Paisley. English, c. 1770, resist dyed. 100% cotton, glazed. 38" wide, 13 1/2" repeat. Document privately owned. No. 6216-11 (blue)

Resist Print. English, c. 1776, resist print. In Montgomery, Printed Textiles, fig. 191 (Pheasants). 100% linen. 50" wide, 26" repeat. Document at the Metropolitan Museum of Art, New York City. No. 6218-1 (blue). Fig. 12

Rodney. English, c. 1776, block print. 100% cotton. 36" wide, 34 1/2" repeat. No. 6236-1 (blue, red and brown on tan)

Washington-Franklin Toile. English, c. 1783-1800, copperplate print. In Montgomery, Printed Textiles, fig. 300 (Apotheosis of Benjamin Franklin and George Washington). 100% cotton. 33" wide, 33 1/2" repeat. No. 6012-1 (red)

F. SCHUMACHER & CO.

Brittany Toile. French, mid-18th century, copperplate print. 100% cotton. 54" wide, 36" repeat. Document in the Schumacher Collection. No. 63483 (ciel)

Khyber. Indian, 18th century, madder and indigo block print. 100% cotton. 36" wide, 48 1/2" repeat. Document in the Schumacher Collection. No. 153493 (cream)

14. <u>Philipsburg Manor Resist</u> by Schumacher, 3rd quarter 18th century

15. <u>Bruton Resist</u> by Schumacher, 18th century

Paisley and Lion. Indian, 18th century, madder and indigo block print. 100% linen. 54" wide, 35/36" repeat. Document in the Schumacher Collection. No. 63132 (red and blue)

Philipsburg Manor Resist. English or American, third quarter 18th century, resist dyed. 58% linen, 42% cotton. 54" wide, 31" repeat. Reproduced for Sleepy Hollow Restorations, Inc., Tarrytown, N.Y. No. 65555 (indigo blue). Fig. 14

Rittenhouse Square. English, late 18th century, copperplate print. 100% cotton. 54" wide, 25" repeat. Document in the Museum of History and Technology, Smithsonian Institution, Washington, D.C. No. 67610 (teal)

Warren Toile. French, c. 1780-90, copperplate print. 100% cotton. 50" wide, 35" repeat. Document owned by the Preservation Society of Newport County, Newport, R.I. No. 161322 (brick)

F. SCHUMACHER & CO. Colonial Williamsburg Reproductions

Unless otherwise cited, all documents are in the collections of Colonial Williamsburg, Williamsburg, Va.

Anthesis. English, late 18th century, block print. 100% cotton. 54" wide, 32" repeat. No. 65133 (rose and tobacco)

Bruton Resist. Probably French, 18th century, resist dyed. 100% linen. 54" wide, 13" repeat. No. 63244 (blue and white). Fig. 15

Horse and Fox. English, c. 1770, copperplate print. 100% cotton. 36" wide, 37" repeat. No. 151572 (red and white)

Jones Toile. English, 1761, copperplate print. In Victoria and Albert Museum, English Printed Textiles, pl. 4. 100% cotton. 40" wide, 77" repeat. Document a 19th-century copy used for bed hangings; original design, inscribed "R. Jones, Old Ford, 1761," is the earliest dated copperplate printed textile. No. 1522552 (toile red)

Liverpool Birds. English, c. 1770-75, copperplate print. 100% cotton. 50" wide, 7" repeat. No. 131120 (vert)

Pintado Stripe. French, c. 1775, block print. 100% cotton. 36" wide, 11 1/2" repeat. No. 50732 (red and blue)

Plantation Calico. French, c. 1785, block print. 100% cotton. 50" wide, 13 1/4" repeat. No. 63120 (grass green)

Pleasures of the Farm. French (Jouy), c. 1783, copperplate print from design by Jean Baptiste Huet. In Clouzot, pl. XVIII. 100% cotton. 40" wide, 40" repeat. No. 50428 (royal purple)

Raleigh Tavern Resist. French, late 18th century, resist dyed. 70% linen, 30% cotton. 50" wide, 42" repeat. No. 178164 (blue). Fig. 16

Solomon's Seal. English, c. 1775, copperplate print. 100% cotton. 40" wide, 35 1/2" repeat. Document plate printed at Bromley Hall Factory, Middlesex, England; owned by the Victoria and Albert Museum, London. No. 154864 (blue)

Wood Floral. English, late 18th century, block and roller print. 100% cotton. 54" wide, 16" repeat. No. 65062 (blue and red)

Williamsburg Apples. French, c. 1750-70, block print. 100% linen. 48" wide, 7" repeat. Document originally used for a quilt lining. No. 60142 (brick)

Also available in a printed 100% cotton adaptation, 54" wide. No. 30500

Williamsburg Bellflowers. French or English, late 18th century, block print. 70% linen, 30% cotton. 50" wide, 14" repeat. No. 160552 (red)

Williamsburg Bluebell Stripe. English, c. 1770, block print. 100% cotton. 54" wide, 1 3/4" repeat. No. 66610 series (document colors brown, purple and blue on white)

Williamsburg Diamond Floral. French (Provence), 18th century, block print. 100% cotton. 54" wide, 8" repeat. No. 64714 (rouge)

Williamsburg Floral Bough. French, c. 1785, copperplate print. 100% cotton. 36" wide, 29 1/2" repeat. No. 56465 (red and cream)

Williamsburg Floral Stripe. French, c. 1785-1800, copperplate print. 100% cotton. 36" wide, 12 1/2" repeat. No. 56333 (red on white)

Williamsburg Floral Trails. English, c. 1770, copperplate print. 100% cotton. 54" wide, 32" repeat. Document probably done at Ware Factory, Crayford, Kent, England. No. 60534 (blue on white)

Williamsburg Floribunda. French, c. 1785-1800, block print. 100% cotton. 36" wide, 30 1/2" repeat. No. 153226 (linnet's egg blue)

Williamsburg Flowered Print. French, c. 1780, block print. 100% cotton. 36" wide, 14 1/2" repeat. No. 50670 (blue and green)

Williamsburg Garden Floral. English, c. 1780-90, block print. 100% cotton. 54" wide, 9 1/4" repeat. No. 65085 (document red)

Williamsburg Indian Flowers. English, c. 1760-80, block print. 100% cotton. 54" wide, 12 1/4" repeat. No. 67750 (red and blue)

Williamsburg Iris. English, c. 1780-85, copperplate print. In Montgomery, Printed Textiles, fig. 238 and pl. 23. 100% cotton. 54" wide, 36 1/2" repeat. Original printed at Bromley Hall, Middlesex, England. No. 67760 (document red)

Williamsburg Nosegay. French, 18th century, block print. 100% cotton. 36" wide, 14" repeat. No. 154732 (mulberry)

Williamsburg Pomegranate Resist. Probably French, 18th century, resist dyed. 70% linen, 30% cotton. 50" wide, 20 1/2" repeat. No. 162694 (blue)

WAVERLY FABRICS Old Sturbridge Village Reproductions

Rural Scenes. English, c. 1780-90, copperplate print. 100% cotton. 54" wide, 27" repeat. Document a quilt at Old Sturbridge Village, Mass. No. 681961 (document red)

WOVEN SILK DESIGNS

BRUNSCHWIG & FILS, INC.

Blackwell Lampas. Italian, c. 1740-60. 55% cotton, 45% rayon. 50" wide, 12" repeat. Reproduced for the Henry Francis du Pont Winterthur Museum, Winterthur, Del. No. 68966.01 (peach with blue and chartreuse)

Boscobel Striped Lampas. French, late 18th century. Reproduced for Boscobel Restoration, Inc., Garrison-on-Hudson, N.Y. Document in the Brunschwig Collection. Special order only

Pomegranate Damask. Mid-18th century. 100% rayon. Reproduced for the Museum of Early Southern Decorative Arts, Winston-Salem, N.C.; used in the museum's 1776 Edenton Parlor. No. 10013.02 (sun gold)

Vittel Damask. Mid-18th century. 64% spun rayon, 36% Bemberg. 50" wide, 16" repeat. Reproduced for the Liberty Hall Restoration, Kenansville, N.C. No. 123560.02 (apricot)

OLD WORLD WEAVERS, INC.

Decatur Damask. Italian, 18th century. 80% silk, 20% rayon. 50" wide, 27 1/2" repeat. Color to order. No. A-162-1808-1483

Duquesne. French, 18th century. 40% silk, 60% rayon. 50" wide, 28" repeat. No. S-5203 (gold)

SCALAMANDRÈ SILKS, INC.

Chinoiserie Damask. French or Italian, c. 1760. 100% silk. 50" wide, 43" repeat. Document at the Scalamandrè Museum of Textiles, New York City. No. 1495-4 (green)

Chinoiserie Damask. French, c. 1730. 100% silk. 50" wide, 18" repeat. Document at the Louvre, Paris. No. 2733-9 (ivory and pale blue)

Chinoiserie Damask. English, 18th century. 33% silk, 67% cotton. 51" wide, 22 1/2" repeat. No. 99010-1 (beige and yellow). Fig. 17

Chippendale Damask. Mid-18th century. 100% silk. 50" wide, 13 1/2" repeat. No. 1360-1 (turquoise and blue)

Damask. English, c. 1750. 100% silk. 50" wide, 24 1/2" repeat. Document at the Scalamandrè Museum of Textiles, New York City. No. 1348-3 (claret). Fig. 18

Damask. English, c. 1750. 100% silk. 50" wide, 14" repeat. Document privately owned. No. 2735 (crimson)

XVIII Century Damask. English, 1750. 38% silk, 62% linen. 50" wide, 34" repeat. Document at Gunston Hall, Fairfax County, Va. No. 90022-2 (green and ivory)

Ferronerie Velvet. Italian, c. 1760. 40% silk, 60% cotton. 23" wide. Document at the Philadelphia Museum of Art, Philadelphia. Handmade in Italy, special order only, 10-yard minimum. No. 3154-4 (blue)

French Damask. French, c. 1730. 100% silk. 50" wide, 35" repeat. Document at Musée des Tissus, Paris. No. 360-2 (red)

Georgian Antique Damask. Italian, 17th century. 40% silk, 60% linen. 50" wide, 17" to 25" repeat (variable). Document privately owned. No. 5138-9 (beige)

Louis XV Damask. Italian, c. 1710. 100% silk. 50" wide, 23 1/2" repeat. Document owned by the Villa Farnesi, Florence, Italy. No. 3184-5 (ivory and gold)

Louis XVI Lampas. French, late 18th century. 100% silk. 50" wide, 27" repeat. Document privately owned. No. 535-1 (beige, gold and red). Fig. 19

Love Bird Damask. Italian, 17th century. 50" wide, 18 1/2" repeat. No. 1098-3 (blue)

Pottsgrove Damask. French, 18th century. 100% silk. 50" wide, 17" repeat. No. 166-1 (gold). Fig. 20

F. SCHUMACHER & CO. Colonial Williamsburg Reproductions

Documents are at Colonial Williamsburg, Williamsburg, Va. Most of these designs are available in adaptations with less expensive fibers.

16. <u>Raleigh Tavern Resist</u> by Schumacher, late 18th century

17. <u>Chinoiserie Damask</u> No. 99010 by Scalamandrè, 18th century

Bruton Damask. 100% silk. 54" wide, 23 1/2" repeat. No. 133440 (red)

Gloucester Damask. Mid-18th century. 100% silk. 50" wide, 28 1/4" repeat. No. 136540 (green and gold). Fig. 21

Green Spring Damask Document. Italian, mid-17th century. 100% silk. 54" wide, 8" repeat. No. 34520 (green)

Lord Dunmore Damask. French, c. 1780-90. 100% silk. 50" wide, 18" repeat. No. 30989 (blue)

Ludwell Damask. Early to mid-18th century. 100% silk. 50" wide, 17 1/2" repeat. No. 136544 (blue and silver)

Spotswood. Possibly Spanish, c. 1700. 67% cotton, 33% silk. 54" wide, 8 3/4" repeat. No. 30528 (blue and gold)

Supper Room Lampas. French, c. 1770-80. 100% silk. 50" wide, 55" repeat. No. 31251 (yellow and silver)

Wetherburn's Checque. 100% silk bourette. 52" wide. No. 82720 (gold and teal)

18. <u>Damask</u> No. 1348 by Scalamandrè, c. 1750

19. <u>Louis XVI Lampas</u> by Scalamandrè, late 18th century (Alfred Losch)

20. <u>Pottsgrove Damask</u> by Scalamandrè, 18th century

21. <u>Gloucester Damask</u> by Schumacher, mid-18th century

1790-1815: Changing Taste and Technology

Toward the end of the 18th century and in the early years of the 19th century, the mechanized textile production that came with the Industrial Revolution lowered costs and brought furnishing fabrics, especially printed cottons, within the economic reach of many persons for the first time. Inevitably, fashion followed, and furnishing fabrics began to be used more widely and in greater abundance than they had before. Most fabrics were still imported from England, which had the most advanced textile technology, but merchants also imported French, Indian and Chinese fabrics into the United States. The infant American textile industry was not yet a factor in providing fabrics for home furnishings.

Although wool bed hangings continued to be used during these years, chintz was now regarded as more stylish and had the added advantage of being easily washable. Bed valances were wider than they had been in the 18th century, ranging up to 20 inches, sometimes with added netting or fringes. The most elaborate designs for bed hangings included many additional pieces--extra valances, short curtains, swags and rosettes. Window hangings also evidenced the growing fashion for fabrics. Chintz was favored in parlors and drawing rooms and wools in dining rooms and libraries. Silk continued to be used in wealthier houses. Windows were hung in the French style with straight curtains under valances or swags and festoons. The parlor replaced the bedroom as the location of the most elaborate drapery treatments.

Wool, durable haircloth and leather were used for upholstery. It was also fashionable to cover chair cushions separately in silk or chintz to match window curtains, but silks were never used in more than a few best rooms, even in the most wealthy houses.

In the mid-20th century it was common to regard pale colors as characteristic of this period. More recent research has shown instead a marked preference for dramatic printed designs and strong, almost glaring colors: rich yellow, orange, scarlet and blue, often arranged in bold combinations. An example typical of this taste is Osterley, an English glazed cotton block print reproduced in document yellow by Brunschwig & Fils (p. 33, fig. 22).

The range of reproduction fabrics available for this period is large, reflecting current interest in the early printed designs.

PRINTS

BRUNSCHWIG & FILS, INC.

Chantecler. French, late 18th century, yellow and madder block print. 41% cotton, 59% flax. 54" wide, 27 3/4" repeat. Document in the Brunschwig Collection. No. 73683.04 (gold)

Chinese Strawberries. English, late 18th century, block print. 100% cotton. 50" wide, 17" repeat. Reproduced for the Wright-Stanly House, New Bern, N.C. Document in the Brunschwig Collection. No. 72353.04 (mauve on yellow)

English Leopard. English, c. 1810, roller print. 100% cotton, glazed. 53 1/2" wide, 13 1/4" repeat. Reproduced for the Henry Francis du Pont Winterthur Museum, Winterthur, Del. No. 77432.04 (teal)

The Hunting Toile. French, late 18th century, resist dyed. 30% cotton, 70% flax. 48" wide, 11 1/2" repeat. Reproduced for the Liberty Hall Restoration, Kenansville, N.C. Document in the Musée Historique des Tissus, Mulhouse, France. No. 70931.04 (red and white)

Marlboro Cotton Print. English, c. 1805-07, block print. 100% cotton. 54" wide, 11 1/4" repeat. Reproduced for the Henry Francis du Pont Winterthur Museum, Winterthur, Del. No. 77183.04 (aubergine and gold). Fig. 2

Mary Anna. French, early 19th century, block print. 100% cotton. 48" wide, 2 1/2" repeat. Reproduced for the Bybee-Howell House, Portland, Ore. Document in the Brunschwig Collection. No. 72445.04 (pink on white)

New Zinnia Toile. French or English, late 18th century, copperplate print. 100% cotton. 55" wide, 39 1/2" repeat. Document privately owned. No. 67272.01 (blue)

Ogden House. English, c. 1814, block print. 100% cotton, glazed. 33" wide, 15 1/2" repeat (original design slightly diminished). Document in the Brunschwig Collection. No. 77778.04 (multicolor on yellow, special order only)

Osterley. English, c. 1805, block print. 100% cotton, glazed. 45 1/2" wide plus one 8 1/2" border on one side, 14 1/4" repeat. Document in the Brunschwig Collection. Original curtains made of this fabric are in the collections of the Victoria and Albert Museum, London, and Old Sturbridge Village, Mass. No. 77063.04 (yellow). Fig. 22

Oxford Chintz. English, c. 1815, block print. In Montgomery, Printed Textiles, fig. 144. 100% cotton, glazed. 48" wide, 12 3/4" repeat. Document owned by the Museum of Early Southern Decorative Arts, Winston-Salem, N.C. Reproduction used in the museum's Oxford Bedroom, c. 1815. No. 75323.04 (coral on saffron). Fig. 23

Pillement Toile. French, late 18th century, copperplate print. 100% cotton. 39" wide, 17 1/2" repeat. Document privately owned. No. 65161.01 (red)

Salem Tavern Stripe. Possibly American, late 18th century, block print. 100% cotton. 48" wide, 1" repeat. Reproduced for the Museum of Early Southern Decorative Arts, Winston-Salem, N.C. Document a woman's pocket found in North Carolina. No. 73358.04 (brown and beige on white)

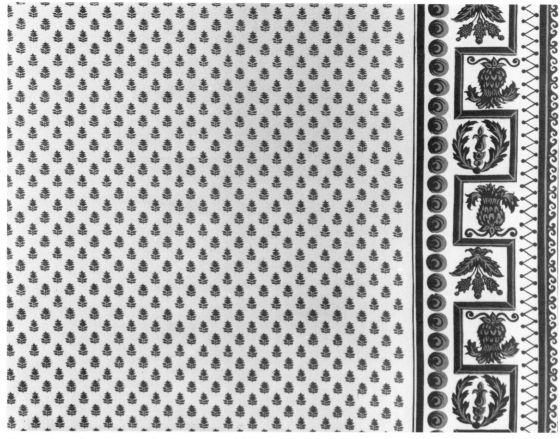

22. <u>Osterley</u> by Brunschwig, c. 1805

23. <u>Oxford Chintz</u> by Brunschwig, c. 1815

Shell Toile. English, late 18th century, copperplate print. In Montgomery, Printed Textiles, fig. 242. 100% cotton. 54" wide, 32 1/2" repeat. Reproduced for the Liberty Hall Restoration, Kenansville, N.C. Document found in Connecticut; now in the Brunschwig Collection. No. 72178.04 (brown on white). Fig. 24

Villeroy. French, c. 1800, block print. 56% cotton, 44% linen. 48" wide, 12 1/2" repeat. Document in the Brunschwig Collection. No. 73930.04 (red and white, special order only)

Wyeth Country. French, early 19th century, block print. 100% cotton. 48" wide, 13 1/4" repeat. Reproduced for the Bybee-Howell House, Portland, Ore. Document in the Brunschwig Collection. No. 73491.04 (blue on red)

SCALAMANDRÈ SILKS, INC.

Andrew Jackson Chintz. English, late 18th century, block print. 100% cotton. 50" wide, 36" repeat. Document found at The Hermitage, Nashville; now at the Scalamandrè Museum of Textiles, New York City. No. 6046-1 (red, blue and green on brown). Fig. 25

Aphrodite Print. English, c. 1790, copperplate print. 48" wide, 32 1/2" repeat. 100% linen. Document used by Thomas Jefferson at Monticello, Charlottesville, Va. No. 6281-10 (document color red)

Adaptation in 100% cotton. No. 6281-5 (black on white)

Blind Man's Bluff. English, late 18th century, copperplate print. 100% linen. 50" wide, 32" repeat. Document privately owned. No. 6065-1 (brown on white)

Directoire Toile. French (Jouy), c. 1805, design by Jean Baptiste Huet. In Clouzot, pl. XXX (Classic Medallions). 100% cotton. 50" wide, 14" repeat. No. 6447-1 (red)

Documentary Print. English, c. 1790, block print. 100% linen. 42" wide, 34" repeat. No. 6295-10 (pink, red and brown on beige)

Floral Design. English, late 18th century, block print. 100% cotton, glazed. 48" wide, 26 3/4" repeat. Adaptation from a document in the textile collection of the Metropolitan Museum of Art, New York City. No. 6533-1 (multicolor blue, rust, yellow and green on white)

Lotus Leaf. French, late 18th century, block print. 100% cotton. 48" wide, 12 3/4" repeat. No. 6439-1 1/2 (blue and gold)

Metropolitan Pomegranate. English, late 18th century, block print. 100% cotton, glazed. 48" wide, 32 1/2" repeat. Adaptation from a document in the textile collection of the Metropolitan Museum of Art, New York City. No. 6408-1 (red, aqua and brown on ecru)

Monticello Stripe. English, c. 1800, block print. 100% cotton. 48" wide, 4 1/2" repeat. Document found at Monticello, Charlottesville, Va. No. 6313-1 (maroon and white)

Oriental Diversions. French, late 18th century, block print. 100% cotton, glazed. 48" wide, 15 5/8" repeat. Document in the Scalamandrè Collection. No. 6405-1 (rose, blue and green on brown)

Quail Unglazed Chintz. English, c. 1815-30, block print. 100% cotton. 47" wide, 15 1/2" repeat. Document at the Scalamandrè Museum of Textiles, New York City. No. 6256-1 (multicolor). Fig. 26

24. <u>Shell Toile</u> by Brunschwig, late 18th century

25. <u>Andrew Jackson Chintz</u> by Scalamandrè, late 18th century

Summer Flora. English, late 18th century, block print. 100% cotton. 48" wide, 11" repeat. Adaptation from a document in the textile collection of the Metropolitan Museum of Art, New York City. No. 6401-1 (red and blue on ecru)

Wilton House Floral. English, c. 1810-25, block print. 100% cotton, glazed. 49" wide, 15 1/2" repeat. Screen printed from a document at Wilton House, Richmond, Va. No. 6364-1 (multi reds and greens on dark brown)

Wilton Phoenix Bird. English, c. 1810-25, block print. 100% cotton. 47 1/2" wide, 13" repeat. Screen printed from a document at Wilton House, Richmond, Va. No. 6349-3 (multicolor on brown)

Woodbury Print. English, early 19th century. 100% cotton. 40" wide, 26" repeat. Document in the American Wing, Metropolitan Museum of Art, New York City. No. 6673-1 (blue and white)

F. SCHUMACHER & CO. Colonial Williamsburg Reproductions

Unless otherwise cited, documents are in the collection of Colonial Williamsburg, Williamsburg, Va.

Williamsburg Bellflowers. French (Nantes), c. 1800, block print. 70% linen, 30% cotton. 50" wide, 14" repeat. No. 160552 (document red and blue)

Williamsburg Flowering Tree. English, c. 1800, block print. 100% cotton. 54" wide, 34" repeat. Document a quilt. No. 60362 (ruby)

Williamsburg Grapes. English, c. 1790, block print. 100% cotton. 54" wide, 17" repeat. Document in the Schumacher Collection. No. 64926 (rust)

Williamsburg Potpourri. English, c. 1815, block print blue, red and brown on white. 100% cotton. 36" wide, 22 1/4" repeat. Adaptation of a document in the Victoria and Albert Museum, London. No. 153033 (buff)

Williamsburg Wildflowers. French, c. 1790, block print. 100% cotton. 50" wide, 31" repeat. Document a coverlet. No. 174443 (multicolor on natural)

Williamsburg Wythe House Border Resist. English or American, late 18th century, resist dyed in two shades of blue on white. 100% cotton. 50" wide, 28" repeat. No. 162544 (blue)

WAVERLY FABRICS Old Sturbridge Village Reproductions

Brookfield Flowers. English, c. 1810, block print. 100% cotton. 54" wide, 12" repeat. Document at Old Sturbridge Village, Mass. No. 681421 (red)

Peel Document. English, 1798, block print. 100% cotton. 54" wide, 24" repeat. Document an unwashed bolt-end bearing the date 1798, English tax marks and the name of the manufacturer, Peel & Co., Sawley, Lancashire, England; at Old Sturbridge Village, Mass. No. 681091 (lacquer). Figs. 1, 27

1795 Floral Stripe. English, c. 1795, block print. 100% cotton. 54" wide, 27" repeat. Document shows flowers in madder colors with blue on alternating dark and light stripes; at Old Sturbridge Village, Mass. No. 681065 (teakwood)

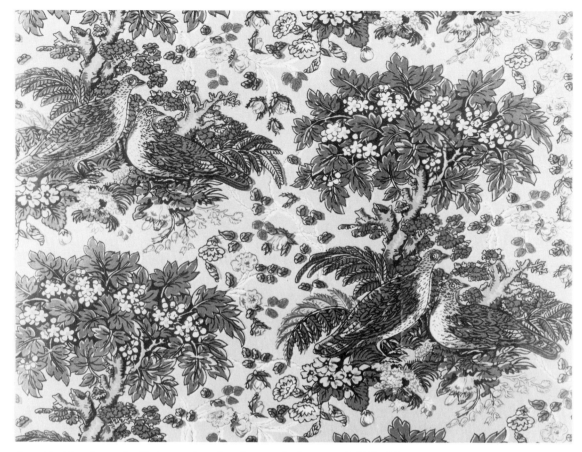

26. <u>Quail Unglazed Chintz</u> by Scalamandrè, c. 1815-30

27. The original fabric from which <u>Peel Document</u> was reproduced by Waverly. Bolt-end with manufacturer's label and English tax stamps, 1798 (Old Sturbridge Village Photo, Donald F. Eaton)

WOVEN DESIGNS

BRUNSCHWIG & FILS, INC.

Baltimore Stripe. European, 1790-1831. 100% rayon. 50" wide. Reproduced for the Henry Francis du Pont Winterthur Museum, Winterthur, Del. No. 64895.01 (pink and green)

Beaumaris Lampas. French, late 18th century. 77% spun rayon, 23% rayon. 50" wide. From a Louis XVI silk document. Reproduced for Boscobel Restoration, Inc., Garrison-on-Hudson, N.Y. No. 32244.01 (pink and green)

Laureal Damask. European, late 18th century. 28% silk, 72% cotton. 52" wide, 27" repeat. Reproduced for the Museum of Early Southern Decorative Arts, Winston-Salem, N.C. No. 11403.02 (bronze)

Also available in 100% rayon. 52" wide, 27" repeat. No. 10006.02 (coral)

Lesparre. French, early 19th century, woven stripe. 100% rayon. 48" wide. Reproduced for the Liberty Hall Restoration, Kenansville, N.C. Document privately owned. No. 30942.00 (blue and cream)

Urn Damask. French, late 18th century. Reproduced for Boscobel Restoration, Inc., Garrison-on-Hudson, N.Y. Woven from the original cards, special order only

SCALAMANDRÈ SILKS, INC.

Adam Damask. English, late 18th century. 100% silk. 50" wide, 18" repeat. Document at Monticello, Charlottesville, Va. No. 1384-6 (crimson). Fig. 28

Empire Lampas. French, c. 1805. 41% silk, 59% cotton. 50" wide, 16" repeat. Gold on red. Reproduction used in the White House, Washington, D.C. Document privately owned. No. 97052-1 (yardage), No. 97053-1 (chair seat), No. 97055-1 (sofa panel)

Federal Lampas. French, early 19th century. 41% silk, 59% cotton. 50" wide, 7 1/4" repeat. Star design. No. 1951-1, special order only

Louis XVI Lampas. French, late 18th century. 100% silk. 50" wide, 69" repeat. Document at Monticello, Charlottesville, Va. No. 1496 (blue and silver)

F. SCHUMACHER & CO. Colonial Williamsburg Reproductions

Bruton Damask. French, late 18th century. 100% silk. 50" wide, 23 1/2" repeat. No. 133441 (gold)

Williamsburg Multi Stripe. Late 18th century. 100% cotton. 50" wide. Chevron twill design. No. 81480; No. 132960

WAVERLY FABRICS Old Sturbridge Village Reproductions

Thomas Sheraton Damask. English (?), early 19th century. 48" wide, 3 1/4" repeat. 100% cotton. Document a scarlet wool window curtain at Old Sturbridge Village, Mass. No. 642287 (scarlet)

1815-1840: Technological Changes and Complex Designs

During the years 1815-40, the development of power looms, the perfection of roller printing and improvements in dye technology greatly changed the textile industry in Europe and the United States and influenced textile fashions as well. Colorful, relatively inexpensive cotton prints were everywhere available for use as bed and window coverings and as slipcovers. Because of the quality of design and printing, even the simplest curtain designs with these furniture chintzes could be regarded as stylish. The use of metal cylinders for printing meant that repeats were smaller and details often very finely wrought. Popular designs included monochromatic landscapes, combinations of block and roller printing, floral stripes and elaborately foliated pillar prints. (For more details see Montgomery, Printed Textiles, pp. 287-342.)

Paintings of the period that include interior views provide useful examples of American fabric furnishings. In wealthier houses, European designs for draperies and valances in silk, wool and chintz were often adapted from English and French publications, as discussed in Samuel J. Dornsife's "Design Sources for Nineteenth-Century Window Hangings." One source was Rudolph Ackermann's monthly periodical Repository of Arts, Literature, Commerce, Manufactures, Fashion and Politics (London, 1809-28), which included colorful plates of curtain and furniture designs, as well as samples of textiles with suggestions for their use. Designs were also included in books such as Pierre de la Mesangere's Meubles et objets de goût and George Smith's A Collection of Designs for Household Furniture. Sheer undercurtains were sometimes added to window treatments as part of a growing taste for layers of contrasting fabrics. In more modest houses, elaborate designs were copied in less expensive fabrics. Curtains continued to be regarded as functional despite the increasing complexity of the designs. They were opened and closed daily to admit or exclude light or air. As late as 1840 the windows of many kitchens and lesser bedrooms were without fabric hangings.

The use of bed hangings during this period was a matter of individual choice that reflected patterns of fashion as well as philosophies of hygiene. Throughout the 1830s and 40s controversy raged over the healthfulness of hangings that enclosed the bed. In 1839 Sarah Josepha Hale, editor of Godey's Lady's Book, wrote, "Bed hangings are unhealthy. They confine the air about us while we sleep." At the same time designers and decorators were publishing new designs for hangings and they were being manufactured in large quantities. It was not until the mid-19th century that bed hangings were relegated to strictly decorative display on the posts and tester frame.

PRINTS

BRUNSCHWIG & FILS, INC.

Boscobel Clover. French, c. 1830, roller print. 100% cotton. 49 1/2" wide plus one 4 1/2" border on one side, 7 1/2" repeat. Document owned by Boscobel Restoration, Inc., Garrison-on-Hudson, N.Y. No. 76232.04 (blue)

Chinese Leopard Toile. French, c. 1825, roller print. 100% cotton. 36" wide, 15 1/4" repeat. Document privately owned. No. 70121.04 (shades of red and blue)

Custom House Glazed Chintz. English, c. 1820-30, roller print. 100% cotton, glazed. 55" wide, 12 1/2" repeat. Document owned by the Society for the Preservation of Long Island Antiquities, Setauket, N.Y. No. 77058.04 (brown and apricot)

Mrs. Fitzherbert Stripe. English, c. 1830, roller print. 100% cotton. 50" wide, 15" repeat. Document in the Victoria and Albert Museum, London. No. 67980.01 (multicolor)

Oriole. English, c. 1830, roller print. In Montgomery, Printed Textiles, fig. 380. 100% cotton. 48" wide, 15 1/4" repeat. Reproduced for the Henry Francis du Pont Winterthur Museum, Winterthur, Del. No. 65810.01 (red and black with yellow and green on tan ground)

Rose Hill Glazed Chintz. French, c. 1830, roller print. 100% cotton. 48" wide, 29 1/2" repeat. Document privately owned at Mulhouse, France. No. 76020.04 (pink, green and turquoise)

Trilport. English or French, c. 1830, block print. 100% cotton.

48" wide, 23 1/4" repeat. Document in the Brunschwig Collection. No. 75120.04 (red and blue)

CLARENCE HOUSE

Rose Cumming Chintz. English, c. 1830-45, block print. 100% cotton. 51" wide, 35 1/2" repeat. Hand blocked in England. No. 31410/01 (multicolor on ice)

Tudor Rose. English, c. 1830-50, block print. 100% cotton. 51" wide, 24" repeat. Hand blocked in England. No. 192650 (red)

GREEFF FABRICS, INC.

Alcott. English, c. 1830, roller print. 100% cotton. 36" wide, 15 1/2" repeat. No. 73062 (red and brown)

OKEN FABRICS

Handprinted Glazed Chintz. English, c. 1825-40. 100% cotton, glazed. 50" wide, 18 1/2" repeat. No. K 2732-1 (nile)

SCALAMANDRÈ SILKS, INC.

Irish Countryside. English, early 19th century. 100% cotton. 50" wide, 25" repeat. Document at the Philadelphia Museum of Art, Philadelphia. No. 6248-4 (blue and white)

F. SCHUMACHER & CO.

Barker Stripe. English, c. 1830, roller and block print. 100% cotton. 54" wide, 19 1/2" repeat. Reproduced for the Preservation Society of Newport County, Newport, R.I. No. 63883 (red and blue on tea ground). Fig. 29

WAVERLY FABRICS Old Sturbridge Village
Reproductions

Fenno House Chintz. English,
c. 1820, roller and block print.
100% cotton, glazed. 54" wide,
22 1/2" repeat. Document at Old
Sturbridge Village, Mass. No. 681041
(tobacco)

Richardson Chintz. English, c. 1820-
25, roller print. 100% cotton,
glazed. 54" wide, 27" repeat.
Document a bedspread at Old Sturbridge Village, Mass. No. 681152
(federal blue)

Sturbridge Document. English,
c. 1825-35, block and roller print.
100% cotton, glazed. 54" wide,
13 1/2" repeat. Document at Old
Sturbridge Village, Mass. No. 681211
(plum)

J. H. THORP & CO.

Mendham Printed Chintz. English,
c. 1820-40, block print. 100% cotton,
glazed. 36" wide, 21 1/4" repeat.
No. T 25123 (gold)

Old English Chintz. English, mid-
19th century, block print. 100%
cotton, glazed. 50" wide, 36 1/2"
repeat. No. T 12441 (ivory)

Handblocked Chintz. English,
c. 1830-50, block print. 100%
cotton, glazed. 50" wide, 20"
repeat. Hand blocked in England.
No. T 22608 (yellow)

WOVEN DESIGNS

BRUNSCHWIG & FILS, INC.

Davout Snowflake Lampas. French,
early 19th century. 51% silk, 49%
cotton. 48" wide, 8 1/4" repeat.
Reproduced for the Chillman Empire

Parlor, Bayou Bend Collection,
Houston, Tex. Document in the
Brunschwig Collection. No.
32261.00 (red), No. 32262.00
(blue), No. 32263.00 (gold), No.
32264.00 (green)

Also available as coordinating
chair seat and back; with borders;
with a plain ground.

SCALAMANDRÈ SILKS, INC.

49" Lampas. French, mid-19th
century. 59% cotton, 41% silk.
49" wide, 30 1/2" repeat. Document
at Lyndhurst, Tarrytown, N.Y. No.
97124-1 (gold and orange)

28. <u>Adam Damask</u> by Scalamandrè, late 18th century (Alfred Losch)

29. <u>Barker Stripe</u> by Schumacher, c. 1830

1840-1870: Popularity in Furnishing Fabrics

In the middle years of the 19th century the use of textiles to decorate American houses was lavish, reflecting the great availability of fabrics and the interest women took in the appearance of their domestic environment. Fashionable fabrics included silk, velvet, damask, plain satin and figured chintz. Women often made their own curtains and bed hangings, although professional upholsterers continued to supply the wealthy. Popular manuals and magazines published designs and patterns and offered suggestions for creating decorative effects inexpensively. For example, Sarah Josepha Hale in Godey's Lady's Book and Catharine Beecher in The American Woman's Home and Treatise on Domestic Economy stressed the importance of textiles in embellishing a house, and they provided readers with pictures and practical instructions as guides. Catharine Beecher felt that it was a reflection of good taste if colors within a room matched.

As in the past, designs for window hangings were inspired by historical styles, but during this period different styles were often mixed in the same house. A basic formula for window hangings was sheer undercurtains, heavy side draperies and a valance that might be distinctively Greek, Gothic or Jacobean. Frequently two or three or more fabrics of different color and texture would be combined in a single design with braids, fringe, cords and tassels adding to the rich effects. Samuel J. Dornsife describes some specific examples in "Design Sources for Nineteenth-Century Window Hangings." Similar effects can be achieved today by using silks, wools or velvets in period colors with appropriate braids, fringes and trimmings. Although there are few documentary reproductions available, plain fabrics similar to the originals of the period can be found in the standard textile market.

REPRODUCTIONS OF 1840-70 FABRICS

PRINTS

BRUNSCHWIG & FILS, INC.

Bettina. French, mid-19th century, roller print. 100% cotton. 48" wide, 29 3/4" repeat. Document in the Brunschwig Collection. No. 37811.01 (red and mauve on cream)

Camas Landing. French, mid-19th century, roller print. 100% cotton. 48" wide, 18 3/4" repeat. Repro-duced for the Bybee-Howell House, Portland, Ore. No. 73481.04 (red and yellow on beige)

Chelsea. English, mid-19th century, roller print. 100% cotton. 49 1/2" wide, 13" drop repeat. Document in the Victoria and Albert Museum, London. No. 65642.01 (teal). Fig. 30

Filigree Stripe. English, c. 1835-45, roller print. 100% cotton. 53" wide, 31 1/2" repeat. Reproduction by rotary screen with the design slightly enlarged and with one motif added. Reproduced for the Henry Francis du Pont Winterthur Museum, which owns a document having a pink ground; another document, privately owned, has a green ground. No. 65744.01 (green). Fig. 31

Leopard Stripe. English, mid-19th century, roller print. 100% cotton, glazed. 50" wide, no repeat. Document privately owned. No. 65632.01 (teal)

Le Coudon. French, mid-19th century, block print. 100% cotton. 48" wide, 6" repeat. Document privately owned. No. 73404.04 (red and olive)

Les Bluets. French, mid-19th century. 100% cotton. 48" wide, 14 1/2" repeat. Document in the Brunschwig Collection. No. 75052.04 (blue and white)

Malabar. French, mid-19th century, roller print. 100% cotton. 48" wide, 18 5/8" repeat. Document in the Brunschwig Collection. No. 65150.01 (multicolor on cream)

Roses and Ribbons. American, c. 1860, roller print originally on challis. 100% cotton, glazed. 48" wide, 30" repeat. Document in the Brunschwig Collection. No. 77359.04 (green ribbons on charcoal)

Roses et Lilas. French, mid-19th century, roller print. 100% cotton. 48" wide, 32 1/4" repeat. Document privately owned. No. 37401.01 (pink and blue on off-white)

Sauvie Island Glazed Chintz Border. c. 1850, roller print. 100% cotton. 48" wide (6 borders, each 6 1/2" wide), 6 1/2" repeat. Reproduced for the Bybee-Howell House, Portland, Ore.

Document in the Brunschwig Collection. No. 77608.04 (brown)

Titania Glazed Chintz. French, mid-19th century, block print. 100% cotton, glazed. 52 1/8" wide, 23 3/4" repeat. Document in the Brunschwig Collection. No. 77560.04 (rose and mauve with a blue stripe)

Victorian Garden. English, c. 1850, block print. 100% cotton. 50" wide, 30 1/2" repeat. Reproduced for the Henry Francis du Pont Winterthur Museum, Winterthur, Del. No. 65807.01 (multicolor on mulberry). Fig. 32

ARTHUR H. LEE & JOFA, INC.

Carries a line of glazed, hand-blocked chintz in the mid-19th century English taste (fig. 33). Many are printed with recuttings of period blocks.

STROHEIM & ROMANN

Tudor. English, c. 1840-60, block print. 100% cotton, glazed. 54" wide, 31 1/2" repeat. No. 26454 (pink with blue stripe on cream)

WOVEN DESIGNS

BRUNSCHWIG & FILS, INC.

Marcotte Damask. French, 19th century. 100% silk. 22" wide, 55" repeat. Reproduced for the American Wing, Metropolitan Museum of Art, New York City; reproduction used for upholstery in the museum's "19th-Century America" exhibit. Special order only

Roanne Silk Damask. Mid-19th century. 100% silk. 48" wide, 19 1/2" repeat (cut by repeat only). Reproduced for the Belter Parlor (1845-70), the Bayou Bend Collection, Houston, Tex. No. 31620.00 series (document color rose)

30. <u>Chelsea</u> by Brunschwig, mid-19th century

31. <u>Filigree Stripe</u> by Brunschwig, c. 1835-45

32. <u>Victorian Garden</u> by Brunschwig, c. 1850

33. <u>Hollyhock</u> by Lee & Jofa, mid-19th century

<u>Victoria Damask</u>. English, c. 1840,
woven. 12% rayon, 58% cotton, 30%
wool. Document wool draperies found
on a Virginia plantation; now in the
Valentine Museum, Richmond, Va.
No. 10705.02 (pink). Fig. 34

OLD WORLD WEAVERS, INC.

<u>Brocatello Museo</u>. Probably Italian,
mid-19th century. 96% silk, 4% linen.
50" wide, 3 3/4" repeat. Reproduced
for the American Wing, Metropolitan
Museum of Art, New York City.
No. A-2474 (royal blue and gold)

EMBROIDERIES

E.C. CARTER CO., order through Greeff
Fabrics, Inc.

Has tambour and appliqué on net and
muslin panels and yardage that are
appropriate for restoration work.

HENRY CASSEN, INC.

Specializes in tambour and appliqué
on both net and cloth drapery panels
and yardage; carries excellent
reproductions of late 19th-century
Corneley embroideries.

1870-1900: Complexity and Variety

During the years 1870-1900 rich and varied combinations of textures, colors and patterns characterized fabric furnishings. The photographs in William Seale's book The Tasteful Interlude record the lavish use of fabrics that extended to upholstered footstools, pillows, portieres and the draping of pianos, tables and chairs. The prominent display of crocheted doilies and elaborate embroideries evidenced a taste for handwork that was promoted by women's magazines and manuals as well as by the values of the English Arts and Crafts movement. Drapery design was exceedingly complex, often utilizing embroidered or lace undercurtains and elaborate fringes, tassels and tiebacks. Plush, sateen, brocatelle, twilled wool, velvets and silks were among the popular fabrics.

During this period the design and use of furnishing fabrics reflected several new influences. From England came the distinctive flat patterned fabrics and wallpapers designed by William Morris' Arts and Crafts firm, as well as an attention to materials and fine craftsmanship. At the same time, stimulated by the United States centennial, there was a revival of American colonial and Federal period motifs, including early reproductions of 18th-century fabrics. For this reason some of the reproductions of 18th-century fabrics that are available today, especially those of French copperplate prints, are as appropriate for late 19th-century interiors as they are for 18th-century ones. A third influence on interior decoration and fabric design that should be noted, although currently it is not represented among reproduction fabrics, was the interest in exotic Japanese and Turkish motifs.

The limited number of late 19th-century documentary reproductions indicates the recent date of interest in this period. There are fabrics on the commercial market that are appropriate for restoration work, and patterns for handwork can be found in contemporary manuals such as The Dictionary of Needlework and in contemporary women's magazines. A successful restoration for this period might rest on a careful selection of drapery accessories combined with appropriate plain fabrics in period colors. There is also always the possibility of custom reproduction (fig. 36). As with all periods, the more familiar one becomes with the prevailing taste, the wider the choice of fabrics that can be used to approximate period effects. Photographs and popular magazines from the late 19th century, such as Harper's and the Ladies' Home Journal, are useful guides to the taste of this period.

REPRODUCTIONS OF 1870-1900 FABRICS

BRUNSCHWIG & FILS, INC.

Dr. Thorton's Tulips. English, late 19th century, roller print. 100% cotton, glazed. 48" wide, 21" repeat.

Document in the Brunschwig Collection. No. 76248.04 (green, brown and cream)

Les Papillons Exotiques. French, late 19th century, roller print. 100%

cotton. 51" wide, 17" repeat. Document privately owned. No. 173418.00 (multicolor on brown)

Narcissus. American, c. 1885-90, block print from design by Candace Wheeler. 100% cotton. 54" wide, 15 1/2" repeat. Adaptation of 100% linen original. No. 72264.04 (green, yellow and white)

Available in 100% linen by special order only. Fig. 35

OLD WORLD WEAVERS, INC.

Damasco Imberline. Italian, late 19th century. 80% silk, 20% cotton. 50" wide, 25" drop repeat. No. A-603-862-3

STROHEIM & ROMANN

Imports from England some of the Arthur Sanderson, Ltd., reproductions of William Morris prints. Occasionally these may also be found in department store drapery departments.

J.H. THORP & CO.

Chintz. English, c. 1870-90, block print. 100% cotton. 50" wide, 37" repeat. Hand blocked. No. T-23220 series

WAVERLY FABRICS Old Sturbridge Village Reproductions

Centennial Patchwork. New England, 1876, roller print. 100% cotton. 54" wide, 18" repeat. Document at Old Sturbridge Village, Mass. No. 681011 (document red)

34. Victoria Damask by Brunschwig, c. 1840

35. Narcissus by Brunschwig, c. 1885-90

36. Silk draperies, tassels, fringes, cords and tiebacks in the Richardson-Bates House, Oswego, N.Y. Custom reproduced by Scalamandrè from the late 19th-century originals (P. Shaefer)

Nondocumentary and Plain Woven Fabrics

Some modern textiles that have changed little or not at all from the originals of an earlier date are entirely appropriate for restoration work. Sources for some of these fabrics--including plain woven checks, cottons and linens and also baize, diaper, dimity and horsehair--are listed in the section that follows. In addition, one should feel free to search elsewhere for period fabrics that are still being manufactured. Identification of the original date and source of such fabrics is sometimes difficult. The best procedure is to note the name of the design and any additional information printed on the selvedge, and then to contact the manufacturer about any documentary information available.

BAIZE

This thin, long-napped woolen cloth was used frequently in the 18th and 19th centuries as a table covering. It is significantly different in texture from modern felt. An acceptable similar fabric is available from:

SCALAMANDRÈ SILKS, INC.

Shelbourne Casement. 50% wool, 50% cotton. No. 99412-5 (green)

Scalamandrè also offers an excellent documentary reproduction, Baize Cloth No. 99243 (see p. 14).

CHECKS

Plain woven checks of either cotton or linen have changed little in the last 200 years. Regular or irregular patterns of squares were used for bed and window curtains as well as for loose cases or slipcovers for furniture. To judge from surviving examples, the most common color was blue, although red, green and brown were also used. Until the mid-19th century, the texture was considerably heavier than that of modern commercial ginghams. A number of textile firms carry checked fabrics as part of their regular stock. In addition there are some museum reproduction checks available:

F. SCHUMACHER & CO. Colonial Williamsburg Reproductions

Unless otherwise cited, documents are in the collection of Colonial Williamsburg, Williamsburg, Va.

Edinburgh Check. 100% linen. 48" wide. No. 83174 (blue)

Tavern Check. 18th century. 61% linen, 39% cotton. 48" wide, 3" squares. Document a linen case for a settee cushion. No. 81508 (document blue). Fig. 37

Williamsburg Check. 18th or early 19th century. 55% linen, 45% cotton. 48" wide, 1/2" squares. No. 118880 series

WAVERLY FABRICS Old Sturbridge Village
Reproductions

Sturbridge Check. American, c. 1810-
30. 50% cotton, 50% polyester.
48" wide, 3/4" repeat. Document a
linen apron at Old Sturbridge Village,
Mass. No. 641968 (blue)

Sturbridge Plaid. American, c. 1810-
50. 50% cotton, 50% polyester.
48" wide, 1 1/2" repeat. Document a
cotton bolster cover at Old Sturbridge
Village, Mass. No. 642268 (blue)

COTTONS

Plain woven cottons are available from
a number of manufacturers, but
inexpensive yardage can often be found
in department stores, sometimes being
sold as lining fabric. Plain glazed
chintzes are also often available in
department store drapery departments.
Firms specializing in fine plain
cottons include:

E.C. CARTER CO. (Swiss imports, order
through Greeff Fabrics, Inc.)

Batiste. 100% cotton. No. 865
(45" wide, white). No. 30529
(44" wide, white). No. 30474
(44" wide, white)

Embroidered Batiste. 100% cotton.
43" wide. No. 30534 (white)

Organdy. 100% cotton. 44" wide.
No. 30106 (white)

Dotted Swiss. 50% cotton, 50% Kodel
polyester. 44" wide. No. 30483
(white)

Vertical Dotted Swiss. 50% cotton,
50% polyester. 44/45" wide.
No. 1500 (white)

37. Tavern Check by Schumacher, 18th century

Also available are a variety of patterns of plain and embroidered cotton yardage and embroidered and lace curtain panels that are suitable for restoration work.

GREEFF FABRICS, INC.

Carousel Glazed Chintz. 100% cotton. 50" wide. No. 126280 series

HENRY CASSEN, INC.

Batiste. 100% cotton. 45" wide. Imported from Switzerland. No. 1590 (white). No. 1594 (ecru)

Dotted Swiss. 35% cotton, 65% polyester. 45" wide. No. 70590 (white)

Organdy. 100% cotton. Imported from Switzerland. No. 1322 (43" wide, white). No. 3263 (68/72" wide, white). No. 3261 (53/54" wide, white)

Henry Cassen, Inc., also carries embroidered and lace curtains and other plain yardage.

WILSON'S, INC.

Offers very inexpensive unbleached 100% cotton tobacco cloth, 36" wide.

COTTON PRINTS

Nineteenth-century printed cotton designs that have never been discontinued are seldom called reproduction fabrics, but some are entirely appropriate for restoration work. Clarence House, Bailey & Griffin and Arthur H. Lee & Jofa have many designs of this type and are helpful in providing documentary information and dating.

DIAPER

In the 18th and early 19th centuries in the United States, diaper referred to pattern-woven cottons and linens that were often used for table covers, napkins and toweling.

Few commercial reproductions of these handwoven goods are currently available, but they can be copied easily by handweavers using published drafts. An excellent selection of drafts is given in Linen Heirlooms by Constance Dann Gallagher. Diaper patterns commercially available are:

SCALAMANDRÈ SILKS, INC.

Cameo Cloth. 100% cotton. 50" wide, no repeat. No. 97711-1 (white)

F. SCHUMACHER & CO. Colonial Williamsburg Reproductions

Williamsburg Dobby Weave. 100% cotton. 54" wide, no repeat. No. 81710 series

DIMITY

In the 18th and early 19th centuries, dimity was a heavy cotton cloth distinguished by various patterns of vertical woven ribs that were regular or irregular. It was used for bed curtains, counterpanes and slipcovers. For modern reproductions contact:

SCALAMANDRÈ SILKS, INC.

Dimity. 100% cotton. 50" wide. Document at Mount Vernon, near Alexandria, Va. No. 1657 (white)

BRUNSCHWIG & FILS has discontinued its Richmond Dimity Cloth but hopes to offer another reproduction dimity soon. Contact the company for more information.

By the late 1820s dimity was also made in a lighter version that was used mainly for clothing. This was called "cap dimity" to distinguish it from heavier "furniture dimity." It too utilized woven ribs as its primary design characteristic, but the cloth was much lighter in weight and the ribs were regularly spaced in rows or checks. Both dimities were available from c. 1825 to 1860. By the late 19th century the lighter dimity was being used for window curtains. It is still available in many department stores.

HORSEHAIR

Beginning in the late 18th century plain and patterned horsehair fabrics in black, red, green and white were frequently used for upholstery. They are carried today by Arthur H. Lee & Jofa, Brunschwig & Fils, Clarence House, Old World Weavers, Peter Schneider's Sons and Scalamandrè. Authentic horsehair fabrics range in width from 25 to 30 inches, restricted by the actual length of the hair. Nylon imitations are usually made wider.

LINENS

HENRY CASSEN, INC.

Handkerchief Linen. 100% linen. 46" wide. No. 4850 (white)

Other linen samples available on request.

F. SCHUMACHER & CO. Colonial Williamsburg Reproductions

Taffeta Linen. 100% linen. 50" wide. Document a linen bedsheet. No. 113887 (natural)

ULSTER WEAVING CO.

Ulster stocks hundreds of types of linen in a variety of textures and widths, including fine cambrics and plain tapes in several widths. The best procedure is to write describing what is wanted and to request samples.

SILKS

Plain and textured silks have never disappeared from production, and many excellent moirés, taffetas and satins are available from companies specializing in drapery fabrics. Brunschwig & Fils, Scalamandrè and Schumacher have designated certain of their patterns as museum reproductions, primarily because of criteria relating to texture. Many other silks are equally suitable for restoration work.

VELVETS

Plain and figured velvets also have scarcely changed. They are available in mohair, cotton, linen and silk from most drapery fabric dealers. Both Clarence House and Brunschwig & Fils can do embossing with 19th-century rollers; several hundred patterns are available. Catalogues illustrating these designs can be consulted in the showrooms.

Washable synthetic velvets are also available. These are not significantly different in appearance, are very durable and cost about one-half as much as silk velvets.

WOOLS

The texture of wools has changed considerably in the past 200 years. For a restoration to a period before the mid-19th century, unless color simulation is the sole criterion, it is advisable to use documentary reproductions of period wools.

Manufacturers

Reproduction Fabrics

Bailey & Griffin, Inc.
227 East 56th Street
New York, N.Y. 10022

Brunschwig & Fils, Inc.
979 Third Avenue
New York, N.Y. 10022

Henry Cassen, Inc.
979 Third Avenue
New York, N.Y. 10022

Clarence House
40 East 57th Street
New York, N.Y. 10022

Greeff Fabrics, Inc.
155 East 56th Street
New York, N.Y. 10022

Lee Behren Silks
Decorators Walk
171 East 56th Street
New York, N.Y. 10022

Arthur H. Lee & Jofa, Inc.
979 Third Avenue
New York, N.Y. 10022

Oken Fabrics
Decorators Walk
171 East 56th Street
New York, N.Y. 10022

Old World Weavers, Inc.
136 East 57th Street
New York, N.Y. 10022

Scalamandrè Silks, Inc.
950 Third Avenue
New York, N.Y. 10022

Peter Schneider's Sons & Co.
Decorators Walk
171 East 56th Street
New York, N.Y. 10022

F. Schumacher & Co.
939 Third Avenue
New York, N.Y. 10022

Stroheim & Romann
155 East 56th Street
New York, N.Y. 10022

J.H. Thorp & Co., Inc.
Decorators Walk
171 East 56th Street
New York, N.Y. 10022

Ulster Weaving Co.
118 Madison Avenue
New York, N.Y. 10016

Waverly Fabrics, Inc.
58 West 40th Street
New York, N.Y. 10018

Additional Source for Trimmings

Standard Trimming Corp.
1114 First Avenue (61st Street)
New York, N.Y. 10021

Tobacco Cloth

Wilson's, Inc.
Department B
258 Main Street
Greenfield, Mass. 01301

Netted Bed Canopies and Edgings

Laura Copenhaver Industries, Inc.
Rosemont
Marion, Va.   24354

Rachel Hawks
Deerfield, Mass.   01342

Mrs. Sheldon Howe
Deerfield, Mass.   01342

Austin Farm House
P.O. Box 815
Richmond, Va.   23207

Leathers

F. Schumacher & Co.
939 Third Avenue
New York, N.Y.   10022

Glossary

The meaning of textile names and the appearance of fabrics themselves have changed over time, making it difficult to know exactly what was meant by a period reference to a fabric. Florence Montgomery is preparing for publication a textile dictionary that will help with many of these problems. Until it appears, the glossary below may help identify fabrics that were intended for household furnishings. For further amplification of period terms, consult dictionaries or encyclopedias of the appropriate period. Two especially helpful works are:

Dickinson, William, ed. <u>A General Commercial Dictionary comprehending trade manufacturers and navigation also agriculture so far as it is connected with commerce</u>. 2d ed., London, 1819.

Beck, S. William. <u>The Draper's Dictionary, a manual of textile fabrics: their history and applications</u>. London, 1882.

BAIZE. Woven woolen cloth having a long nap. Frequently used to cover desk and card table surfaces, either glued down or as a loose cover. Green appears to have been the most common color.

BATISTE. Fine light cotton or linen, usually cotton; from the French word for cambric.

BOURETTE. Silk fabric with a dull finish characterized by random black specks that are actually portions of the silk cocoon.

BROCADE. A figured fabric in which the design is woven in wefts that float on the fabric back or are cut away. These threads appear on the surface only in areas required by the design.

BROCATELLE. A special form of lamps with a pattern in one weave on a contrasting ground. Often heavy silk or linen is used for the ground wefts, which do not appear on the surface of the fabric.

CALAMANCO. A glazed worsted fabric, either plain or woven with a figured design in colors resembling silk brocades.

CALICO. Cotton cloth with patterns printed in one or more colors. In the 18th and early 19th centuries referred to printed cloth imported from India; now usually cotton prints with small stylized patterns.

CAMBRIC. Fine bleached linen.

CAMLET. Unglazed worsted fabric of plain weave. Descriptive of a group of 18th-century materials including harrateen, moreen and china (cheyney). See Hazel E. Cummin, "Camlet," Antiques, December 1942, pp. 309-12.

CHEYNEY. See camlet.

CHINTZ. Glazed cotton cloth, in the 18th century always printed. First manufactured in India, but then imitated elsewhere. Printed designs usually have at least five colors and are frequently large-scale floral patterns.

CRETONNE. A stout unglazed cotton cloth printed on one or both sides, late 19th century in origin. It was used for window curtains and chair covers. At the present time it is unavailable in the United States.

DAMASK. A reversible woven design of contrasting faces. Can be wool, silk or linen.

DIMITY. Cotton cloth with woven ribs forming a pattern of either stripes or checks; also see page 55. For more detail, see Hazel E. Cummin, "What Was Dimity in 1790," Antiques, July 1940, pp. 23-25.

DOCUMENTARY COLORWAY. A modern manufacturers' term used to indicate that the colors of the reproduction fabric are those of the original document. A colorway is a particular printed combination of colors.

DOUBLE WOVEN. Two ply, or made with two layers that are interwoven at regular intervals.

DROP REPEAT. A design that matches motifs in an alternating, zig-zag pattern when joined lengthwise; it requires additional yardage.

FAILLE. A ribbed fabric formed with heavier weft than warp yarns.

FURNITURE. A term commonly used in the 18th century to denote the full equipment of something. A "bed and furniture" meant the mattress, bolster, pillows, sheets, pillowcases and hangings; a "tea table and furniture" referred to a tea table with its accompanying objects for the service of tea. In the case of "window curtain and furniture," furniture referred to the rods, hooks, etc., as well as the cloth.

FURNITURE CHECK. A kind of checked linen or cotton used for slipcovers, window curtains and bed hangings, 18th century to the present.

GAUFRAGE. An embossing technique in which a heated metal cylinder having a raised design on it is pressed against the pile of plain fabric, such as velvet, thereby transferring the pattern.

GLAZED. Having a smooth and lustrous surface coating on the exposed side only.

HARRATEEN. In 18th-century England and colonial America, a wool moiré.

HOLLAND. An 18th and early 19th-century term for closely woven linens, first manufactured in Holland but later throughout the British Isles.

LAMPAS. A figured fabric using additional wefts and warps to form a design in one texture on the ground of another. These additional fibers are woven into the back of the fabric, but it is not reversible.

MARSEILLES. A heavy cotton fabric with a pattern woven in the goods. Usually white, it was primarily used for bed coverings. Marseilles quilts were used from the late 18th century to the early 20th.

MATELASSE. A double-woven cloth that simulated quilting by interlocking in some areas to produce a puckered effect.

MOIRÉ. Fabric, often taffeta, having a surface that appears wavy or watery.

MOREEN. A stout woolen or cotton-wool blend, often embossed with a figured design. Commonly used for upholstery.

MUSLIN. A fine thin cotton cloth with a downy nap on its surface. Generally plain but sometimes decorated with openwork or embroidery. The finer grades were often called mull.

OSNABURG. A kind of coarse linen originally made in Osnabrück, Germany, but later imitated in England and elsewhere. Sometimes spelled "Ozenbriggs."

PALAMPORE. A cotton bed covering from India, usually printed or painted with beautiful designs.

PLUSH. A fabric with an even pile, shorter and less dense than that of velvet. Used for upholstery in the mid to late 19th century.

REPEAT. One complete pattern motif.

RESIST DIE. A method of indigo printing in the 18th century in which a resist paste inhibited the dye. For a full discussion see Montgomery, Printed Textiles, pp. 194-211.

RUSSELL. Ribbed or corded fabric, usually with a cotton warp and wool weft.

SATIN. A shiny fabric created by a special weave leaving floats of numerous warp yarns on the surface. Usually silk, also wool and linen.

SATEEN. A smooth satin weave cloth usually in cotton. Used for window hangings, bed covers and occasionally as a ground for embroidery in the 19th and 20th centuries.

SELVEDGE. The lengthwise edges of a piece of cloth, often of heavier threads and sometimes a different weave intended to prevent raveling.

SLUBS. Lumps on thread, formed by careless spinning. Deliberate use of slubs to give an antique effect to finished cloth is inappropriate for restoration purposes.

STUFF. Commonly a thin woolen cloth.

TAFFETA. A closely woven, firm fabric of even weight and tension, known by its glossy surface. Usually silk but can be linen.

TAMBOUR. Embroidery worked on fine cloth with a small hook forming a chain stitch on the upper surface of the cloth.

TOBACCO CLOTH. Unbleached white cotton cloth used for protecting certain tobacco plants from direct sunlight, thus producing "Shadegrown Tobacco." Resembles the texture and weight of pure cotton muslin.

TOILE. From toile imprimée, meaning printed cotton. Now generally refers to copperplate-printed fabrics, either cotton or linen, more correctly those of French origin.

VELVET. A pile fabric created by the use of an extra warp over rods or wires in loops. It can be plain (left as woven) or the loops can be cut. If the pattern is created by alternating areas of cut and uncut loops, the fabric is called ciselé velvet. If the pattern is woven leaving some areas without pile, it is called voided velvet. Usually wool, silk or cotton.

WARP. The threads that are stretched lengthwise on the loom, usually spun more tightly than the weft.

WEFT. The threads that are interwoven with the warp, thereby running crosswise in the goods, from selvedge to selvedge.

WORSTED. Fabric made of long staple wool that has been combed to make the fibers lie parallel to each other when spun.

Selected Bibliography

This bibliography emphasizes books and articles that are likely to be available in public collections and through interlibrary loan. A more extensive bibliography for the period prior to 1850 can be found in Florence Montgomery, <u>Printed Textiles: English and American Cottons and Linens, 1700-1850</u>.

Adrosko, Rita J. <u>Natural Dyes and Home Dyeing</u>. New York City: Dover Publications, 1971.

Beecher, Catharine, and Stowe, Harriet Beecher. <u>The American Woman's Home</u>. 1869. Reprint. Hartford, Conn.: Stowe-Day Foundation, 1975.

Beer, Alice B. <u>Trade Goods: A Study of Indian Chintz</u>. Washington, D.C.: Smithsonian Institution Press, 1970.

Brightman, Anna. "Window Curtains in Colonial Boston and Salem," <u>Antiques</u>, August 1964, pp. 184-87.

_____. <u>Window Treatments for Historic Houses, 1700-1850</u>. Washington, D.C.: National Trust for Historic Preservation (Preservation Leaflet Series, No. 14), 1968.

_____. "Woolen Window Curtains: Luxury in Colonial Boston and Salem," <u>Antiques</u>, December 1964, pp. 722-27.

Caulfeild, Sophia, and Saward, Blanche C. <u>The Dictionary of Needlework</u>. 1882. Facsimile edition. New York City: Arno Press, 1972.

Clouzot, Henri, and Morris, Frances. <u>Painted and Printed Fabrics</u>. New York City: Metropolitan Museum of Art, 1927.

Cooper, Grace Rogers. <u>The Copp Family Textiles</u>. Washington, D.C.: Smithsonian Institution Press, 1971.

Cummings, Abbott Lowell, ed. <u>Bed Hangings: A Treatise on Fabrics and Styles in the Curtaining of Beds, 1650-1850</u>. Boston: Society for the Preservation of New England Antiquities, 1961.

_____. <u>Rural Household Inventories</u>. Boston: Society for the Preservation of New England Antiquities, 1964.

D'Allemagne, Henry-Rene. <u>La Toile Imprimée et les Indiennes de Traite</u>. 2 vols. Paris: Gruend, 1942.

Dornsife, Samuel J. "Design Sources for Nineteenth-Century Window Hangings," <u>Winterthur Portfolio 10</u>. Charlottesville, Va.: University Press of Virginia, 1975.

Downing, A. J. The Architecture of Country Houses...with remarks on interiors, furniture.... 1850. Reprint. New York City: Dover Publications, 1969.

Eastlake, Charles L. Hints on Household Taste. 4th ed., 1878. Reprint. New York City: Dover Publications, 1969.

Edwards, Ralph, and Ramsey, L.G.G. Connoisseur Period Guides to the Houses, Decorations, Furnishing and Chattels of the Classic Periods. 6 vols. New York City: Reynal, 1957-58. 6 vols. in 1, New York City: Bonanza, 1968.

Fowler, John, and Cornforth, John. English Decoration in the 18th Century. Princeton, N.J.: Pyne Press, 1974.

Gallagher, Constance Dann. Linen Heirlooms. Newton Centre, Mass.: Charles T. Branford Co., 1968.

Little, Francis. Early American Textiles. New York City: Century Company, 1931.

Lubell, Cecil. Textile Collections of the World: United States and Canada. Cincinnati, Ohio: Van Nostrand Reinhold Co., 1976.

Montgomery, Florence. "Antique and Reproduction Furnishing Fabrics in Historic Houses and Period Rooms," Antiques, January 1975, pp. 164-69.

_____. "Eighteenth-Century English and American Furnishing Fashions," Antiques, February 1970, pp. 267-71.

_____. "Furnishing Textiles at the John Brown House, Providence, Rhode Island," Antiques, March 1972, pp. 496-500.

_____. Printed Textiles: English and American Cottons and Linens, 1700-1850. New York City: Viking Press, 1970.

_____. "Upholstery and Furnishings Fabrics" in American Furniture: the Federal Period by Charles F. Montgomery. New York City: Viking Press, 1966.

Peterson, Harold L. Americans at Home. New York City: Scribners, 1971.

Pettit, Florence H. America's Printed and Painted Fabrics, 1600-1900. New York City: Hastings House, 1970.

Praz, Mario. An Illustrated History of Furnishing from the Renaissance to the Twentieth Century. New York City: George Braziller, 1964.

Seale, William. The Tasteful Interlude: American Interiors Through the Camera's Eye, 1860-1917. New York City: Praeger Publishers, 1975.

Thornton, Peter. Baroque and Rococo Silks. New York City: Taplinger Publishing Co., 1965.

Victoria and Albert Museum. English Printed Textiles: Large Picture Book No. 13. London: Her Majesty's Stationery Office, 1960.